TIMELESSNESS
A NEW SETH BOOK

John and Dotti McAuliffe

Uni*Sun
Kansas City

Distribution by The Talman Company.

The Talman Company
150 Fifth Avenue
New York, NY 10011

ISBN #0-912949-22-8
Library of Congress Catalog Card Number 88-051045

A
Uni★Sun
BOOK
Distributed by
THE TALMAN COMPANY

To The Readers,

We wish to thank all of our readers for their friendly support in light of the strange turn of events that have allowed us once more to bring forth Seth. We undertook to write these books when Seth became available to us to share the teaching which has helped us so much. It was with a sense of trepidation that we first proposed to the publisher this unprecedented idea of channeling an entity that was beloved by many, following the death of the former channel. We hope to continue to write more of these books in the future as Seth makes them available.

John & Dotti McAuliffe

TIMELESSNESS

AUTHORS'
PREFACE

John and Dotti came together at a time when their individual growth seemed at a standstill. John was a salesman and Dotti a hair stylist when they met. John was channeling various energies for himself and was the inventor of a few energetic spiritual devices. Upon meeting in San Rafael, California, Dotti wondered why John would keep this information to himself and she proceeded to bring in other individuals for the growth of all.

Their lives took on a completely different path within a year, which brought a close personal relationship. It wasn't long before their jobs were removed and they dedicated themselves to the full time pursuit of spiritual growth. There were three children involved, who were quite surprised to suddenly see the influence of various spiritual entities in their lives.

Soon the voice of a spirit named Kryon was heard in their home, sometimes a little louder than would befit the comfort of all. After some time, Kryon sounded as if he might be borrowing some teachings from another entity. This entity would be known by the name of Seth. After testing the energy at a channeling session, but not identifying himself directly, Seth then emerged and stated that he wished to write another book.

Up until this point, Kryon had introduced Seth prior to his speaking directly through the channel. At this time, Seth started to come through directly and has been active in writing and teaching at various channeling sessions and personal readings.

The use of some of the ideas presented in Seth's books and other private sources of information have enabled John and Dotti to expand their consciousnesses into various modes of seeing and healing that are not even suspected by their neighbors and friends.

Seeking to live the teachings given forth both by Seth, other entities, and meditation, their lives are beginning to take on some of the aspects of ancient civilizations. Healing of mundane physical difficulties has taken itself out of the physical world and into the realms of higher unseen energy. Problems are not addressed in the physical fashion, either, but are assessed as to their relevance to higher information. In short, their lives are leaving the gold oriented approach to material existence and are orienting themselves to freedom from the false goals of the egotistical world.

Their horizons have expanded to include experiments in consciousness involving electronics, astronomy, archaeology of ancient temples, travel and several musical instruments including chimes.

Nearly every room of their house including the garage has some form of geometric and/or electronic instrument in it designed by an aspect of spirit to raise consciousness. Someone once remarked that if you turn on a water faucet, the whole house raises in energy.

Most of the people who come to the various channeling sessions, of which there are some fifteen to twenty-five per week, have known each other for some *time*. They have endeavored to work out their various attachments in the physical realm that generate problems for them. The idea is to generate knowledge from the highest realms obtainable without slipping into "cult judgement" and to assist each other for spiritual growth. An aspect to be avoided at all costs is one of self-righteousness or of being separate from others.

The three children who have lived with John and Dotti have reacted differently to all of these changes. The oldest, Mia, now eighteen, relies trustfully on Seth and other entities for advice in her life. Johnny, now seventeen, has miracles appear all around him, but does not appear to have strong leanings in the spiritual direction. The youngest, Danielle, now twelve, has channeled designs of several spiritual devices including the "fear sponge," made of crystals wired in a specific pattern designed to help alleviate anxieties.

After being associated with Seth and others over a period of time, John and Dotti's horizons of freedom have been expanded and their dreams of travel to exotic locations are being realized. Seth is ardently taking advantage of this interest and continues to use the various ancient temples they see as backdrops in his writing.

As this book was written, the authors actually lived it in such a way that they would begin to understand its concepts. The information in this book has contributed much to bringing them closer and giving them freedom from the emotional stress that formerly would have been driving forces in their lives.

This book is written to help those who are struggling, as the authors have struggled, attempting to overcome traditional and limiting concepts of time that would slow their spiritual growth.

WHAT IS TIME?

Time is understood by beings simply as a measurement which is depicted by a clock. Now, everyone knows this and theoretically, each being in a particular country, in a particular time zone, would be on or within this measurement. There is a problem here already, because the various time zones have artificial boundaries placed on them by simplistic logic, which places artificial limitations on them. So, beings within a particular time zone all have a degree of relative sameness as measured by time. Simplistically, if one stood with one foot on one side of one time zone and one foot on the other side, he would be split in time, wouldn't he?

*"We're only into the first paragraph of this book and I am already in trouble because this question is not as simple as it first appears and I can't answer it."**

If I looked far and wide throughout the earth plane, I couldn't find a better being as an example to illustrate the illusion of time. Of anyone I have ever met, you probably have as different an opinion of it as is available. You are the perfect illustration of the illusion. I hope you're not offended.

(Seth calls in my daughter, Mia, and asks her the same question.)

*Editor's note: John channels Seth while Dotti records her conversations with him. Her responses and observations are in italics.

Mia, as I stand across this theoretical border in time, which Seth would you talk to, the one in 8:00 PM or the one in 9:00 PM?

Mia says, "I will talk to the 8:00 PM Seth because I like even numbers."

All right, Mia, I will jump over to 9:00 PM and you may speak to me there. What is the difference?

Mia replies, "But, Seth, it is the same."

Seth says, "What do you mean?"

Mia answers, "There is no boundary. It doesn't exist."

"I know," Seth replies. "It is an illusion."

Mia says, "It is where the sun is focused."

"You mean," Seth answers, "as I jump back and forth, I can pull the sun with me across the line?"

"No, that's not what I mean," Mia says, "I think I'll go meditate."

"It would make more sense if we were hundreds of miles apart."

It would?

"Yes, for reasons I cannot explain."

That's all right. No one else can explain them, either. But this seems to be what is known as logic, which makes perfect sense! The question comes to mind, whose logic, yours or mine, or would it be a mythical being? Logic is supposed to make sense, isn't it?

Now, someone might say, "Seth, you are not making any sense here. Everyone knows that you are supposed to have artificial boundaries set up in order to make logical sense out of time. And further, since the sun does not set in lines, then one has to draw one someplace and that's the way it is, so that everyone would understand the rules."

It seems that all things are limited with artificial boundaries in relationship to time. Convenience would dictate that we would have artificial rules imposing artificial limitations. Let us try to examine this. If someone would ask you to show up at a particular time, say 7:00 PM, what would it mean to you?

"Just that we are to meet at 7:00 PM."

What time would you actually arrive?

"I would shoot for 7:00 PM, but I've been known to be late, so I might not make it exactly on time."

(At this point, my daughter, Danielle, comes in and asks the date. I tell her it is the 11th. Seth responds and says that it is the 10th. Something is going on here, as my son, Johnny, just came in and complained about my late night hours and that I sleep too late in the day. He also added that he wasn't getting enough attention, that I have been "spacing him out." This seems to be some kind of a set up.)

What I meant when I asked about the time and you keep putting me off with logical responses, thinking that is what I wish to hear, was that you would show up when the mood struck you. You use time as when you were completed with what you assigned yourself, then that would be the time to arrive. There would be no thought as to traffic, weather conditions or any other factor that might interfere with you arriving at 7:00 PM. 7:00 PM would be when you arrive, not what time the clock said. Is that about accurate?

"Bull's eye!"

Now, there are countries whereby everyone thinks in this way and things are accomplished whenever anyone feels like it. You set your own rules. A bus would arrive whenever someone feels like driving it.

In Western society, then, beings attempt to put great emphasis on a specific, appointed time and equate this to efficiency. Many would start at a certain hour and minute and no matter what state of thinking a being is in, the schedule would be adhered to.

There was a break of a few days until we resumed the book.

Now, as you can see, it is not so easy for you to adhere to the rules of time. For, right after we were discussing this, what happened?

"We were very late for a channelling session in San Francisco and two people we care a lot about were clearly inconvenienced."

And what was the result of this?

"I decided to take a look at what my thoughts on time are."

And what did you conclude from that?

"That I'm oblivious to time."

And why do you think that is? Another way of putting it is, what does time mean to you?

"Somehow, it's a limiting measurement which stops me from doing what I want to do."

You have made a good point in that time is limited, but in a way that the word does not imply. Time, then, is a finite measurement used as a convenience to set an artificial schedule. There is a real schedule, but time has nothing to do with it. In other words, it is timeless. There is a greater power that in fact sets this schedule and it is a matter of energy and knowing, which is helped by learning. Did you know there was always enough time?

"I hear this a lot, but obviously, it is not sinking in."

Time would imply space in its measurement and since this is unlimited in the universe, there would always be enough of it. If you used land as a criteria, then space might be limited. But, if space were included, it would be theoretically unlimited. This is a strange paradox, isn't it? Something is out of balance. If you never run out of space, then it seems that the limited amount of time that is artificially set would

4

have to be set artificially by the ego. Do you know what I mean?

"No."

Then you have the false self setting time. Automatically, if one thought about it in some creative way, if this was possible, one would know that something is wrong here. How could this be? Well, it is the false self setting up artificial limits to keep itself in business. That is to say, it would set a limit of tomorrow this will happen. The false self would say you have to pay rent tomorrow.

"Yes. And the universe has dropped you in the wrong spot because the money isn't there."

Now, the universe being perfect in its knowingness, sees without benefit of time that the overall schedule has all events tying into place in perfect order. When I said without *benefit*, I could as well have said without the hindrance of time. The universe, according to perfect schedule, would have all events fit into place without the slightest consideration for time.

Time is, therefore, a limited focus placed there by the limits of the false self.

Time is also limited in a reverse way. This is to say that time is equal to learning. You use time until you no longer need it to learn lessons which your greater focus has scheduled for you to learn. What does this mean to you?

"That we're not going to pay the rent on time."

All right. Not necessarily, but what I mean is (*Seth laughs*), there is an unlimited amount of time available to you, as much as you need to learn the lessons that you are scheduled to learn.

The only time you are truly happy is when you aren't in time. Do you know that?

"Yes, I know it, but I tend to slip back into time a lot of the time."

To go back to the one example of where you were to be someplace at a fixed time and were late, you can then truly see that time was used to learn a lesson, for both you and the others.

(Seth walks outside and throws a ball to the dog. He sure is wasting time today.)

The others then would teach you something of time, also, wouldn't they? For they have other ways of wasting time, specifically, yours. In effect, all learn from each other.

Obviously, then, in a world set up with artificial limits in time, it would be one that allows the false self to continue functioning and learning. What I meant, then, was when you are truly happy, you are focused right now and you will hear me use this term quite frequently throughout any communication that I might use.

Now, (Seth laughs) if you truly focus on today in the here and now, what would happen tomorrow really has no consequence! The rent comes to mind. Today, you really have plenty of time, for you know not what the universe has scheduled for tomorrow. You can see, then, why this friend of yours speaks of a greater schedule and it would imply universal principals not of time. *(Muffy, our cat, leaps up on Seth's lap and settles in, purring.)* You can see, that your cat is not in time. She enjoys the now moment and does not worry about past or future events. Animals would be your teachers if you would let them. Animals know no consequence of time. When they get hungry, it is now, not later.

Think of all of the times that you might have been unhappy and with each one, you would be thinking of another time. So, time is a focus, only. That is, time is where you are focused at a given moment. Most of those moments are not the now moment, as we have discovered.

You have a friend who invented this device and uses it as an example of the right and left brain. He views this as the lower and upper focuses. The left side or lower side is limited to time and would be limited to rote mathematical calculation and the memory of fixed events. That is, the name of someone, the numerical equivalent to a function or something of a fixed, limited nature. This particular part of the self has a limited degree of imagination, fixed by experience and, in effect, would have the problem of being able to generate limited, fixed solutions. His teaching, with this device, shows one how to shift his focus from the clock oriented, lower self to the timeless realm of creativity in the higher self. By use of this device, with a spinning motion, a being's energy is shifted to a higher, emotionless state whereby the higher focus, out of time, instructs the lower, limited self on how to function in a world that would be bereft of creativity. Once focused from the higher self, a being would be detached from emotion which, coincidently, is attached to results. Once one is removed from the result oriented emotion, one can be free in a timeless fashion to let unlimited intelligence solve one's problems in the most expeditious manner.

The key to this whole idea is the freedom from the memory of fixed events, thereby limiting thinking. In essence, one would propel one's self into knowing and the process of solving a problem is then automatic.

If one could expand his thinking to accommodate a different feeling of time, he would be expansive enough to realize that different beings have different feelings about time. The old adage, time is what you make it,

7

applies here. Beings with a poor understanding of their concept of time put pressure on themselves for not ever being focused in their concept of time. Do you understand this?

"Does this have anything to do with feeling bad about yourself because you're often late?"

This is only a part of it, for your unawareness of your concept of time places you under a great degree of stress. There are many beings on the planet who place themselves under a great degree of stress in that they overestimate what can be accomplished in the time they would allow. This gets to be a habit and what these beings do is race around, constantly under pressure, seeking to beat the time they have mis-created. Yes, miscreated, for they, indeed, have constructed this false concept of time. Why would it be that some beings would efficiently go about their lives pacing time without stress? Are they in a different time? Indeed, they are, for time, as it turns out, is just a focus.

If you are focused in the now moment, then you are not in time. Everyone understands that, I presume. Out of the now moment, however, you could be one of several different focuses and they would all be you. Which one of you, that is focused at a given time would resolve the question of how efficient you are with your time? Are you your angry self? With the distraction that this places upon you, not much would get resolved. Are you your happy self? Then much more would get resolved.

Energy comes into play here. How much energy do you have? If you have a lot of energy, then you might accomplish a great deal more in an expanse of time than at a low period, low energy time or versus another being with greater energy.

8

The year would make a difference, also, for as years ascend in numerical order, energy would gradually be getting greater.* Obviously, then, for convenience, as with mathematics and physics, an arbitrary measurement was adopted. As greater energy comes into play by sheer volition on this planet, use of an artificial measurement becomes less useful and the dawn of greater intelligence comes forth to bring greater understanding. Now, what did I say here?

"We can forget worrying about time and concentrate on being happy."

Not exactly. It is time to explain further that the concept of measuring time needs to be greatly expanded. The reason for this need would be to understand greater parts of yourselves which do not hold to time. Beings tend to regulate their lives strictly to an artificial measurement of time. One needs to work so many hours per day. One needs to sleep so many hours per day. One needs to eat at certain times per day.

If you take the example of you and John, how does the foregoing apply to John, if not you, also?

"If John gets a lot of sleep, he feels good, but if he gets little sleep, he still feels good. If he accomplishes a lot during the day, he feels good and if he accomplishes little, he feels good. He doesn't fall apart if he misses a meal, but enjoys the meals he has. John feels good all the time and doesn't worry about time."

What have you just discovered here?

"Some of the differences between John and I."

That wasn't exactly what I had in mind. What I meant was, you have described someone who has a different concept of time than you and most beings do. Now, he wears a watch, which would indicate that he uses

*This does not refer to the age of beings.

9

it from time to time. (*Seth laughs.*) But it seems that it means something different to him than others. It is more of a universal time or a greater use of timelessness, isn't it? Do you suppose that he is going at a different rate of time than others?

"It would seem so."

This can be taught to other beings. John has this friend, you see, who taught it to him. This concept of non-time reduces stress and produces greater energy, doesn't it? I am not certain you are getting what I am suggesting.

"I know what he's got, but I don't know how he got it. I think it's because he's in the now moment a great deal of the time."

He's in the now moment more than most beings. Do you understand this?

"Yes, this I understand."

You can be in time, then, and not of it. You can have it as your ally, not your enemy. Surprisingly, the reduction of fear brings time into focus. That may seem mystical, but in essence, it is practical because fear takes a lot of time. Emotion takes a lot of time and without the concentration on excess emotion, you have a lot of time left. In effect, then, Time Is What You Make It.

HOW DOES TIME AFFECT US?

Now, one could ask, "How does the sun affect us with its energy?" The measurement known as time, in the Western world, brings one to the realization that its effect would be one of controlling the being. The worry about time takes much time and tends to string it out. That is to say, the very worry about the subject itself would in effect, slow time sometimes to a crawl. It affects nearly every state of your being. You get up in the morning and you want to know the time. The effect of an alarm clock would already hover over you. Think of the many parts of your thought system that are artificially, or you might say "realistically" governed by time. How long do you eat? How long do you sleep? How long do you exercise, work, play, arrive at a movie, avoid traffic at which time? Not only are you affected by this, but all whom you intersect with are on the same relative measurement. If you wish to talk to someone by telephone, you call them at a certain time, not 3:00 AM, unless one was under other strange influences.

If you were not under the artificial restrictions of time, you might be freer to contact one who needed help who might be a friend, at a strange time. Let us say you had a strong feeling that your friend might be in some sort of difficulty at 12:15 AM. Since this was in the parlance of time at a time that it would not be "proper" to call, you might let the opportunity pass by and you and your friend would suffer accordingly. If one could throw out the artificial influence of time, he would find that his internal clock would hold him in good value. In other words, other forces would then start to take hold in a way that their "real programming" would become apparent. Within all beings could be found the remnants of a far superior clock and left to its own devices, would be led in a far happier state of affairs than with the use of the artificial measurement.

If you wished to conduct an experiment, you could set aside a day or two, calling it an experimental vacation. In this experimental vacation, you would allow yourself to let go and have your life flow in a natural way. The natural way is to let happen as you internally deem fit. To set up this artificial scenario, one would restrain his "normal, timed, programmed activities." One of these methods, then, is to sit down in a convenient place with nothing planned and decide to accomplish the first thing that comes to your mind without the effect of time. It might be sleeping, it might be walking or it might be eating or playing a musical instrument. With a bit of practice, different activities or lack thereof would then start presenting themselves. Do not, under any circumstances, believe that any of these should have judgement attached. Any activity or thought could be allowed and thoughts that this is inane or stupid need be thrown out. The next thought, that this is lazy or inefficient, need be thrown out, also. Do you understand what I have in mind here?

"Yes."

What do you think would be accomplished by this?

"A real start at learning to go with the flow."

What else?

"I think you'd find out what you really want to do and probably accomplish the most important things to you, even though you might not realize it."

There is something else that comes to mind with this and that is a loosening of the restrictive chain of time upon your thinking.

What happens to you when you feel the pressure of a time restriction, a deadline?

"I get very stressed and do too much planning. Being a news reporter would probably kill me, even though the actual work would be very exciting. Some people respond to deadlines, but I'm not one of them. Deadline is an appropriate word for something that would probably kill me with stress."

Each moment thought of, in time, would be one out of the now moment. It would be one suggesting movement or action, that which generates from the false self. Now, I am not suggesting that any of this is inappropriate or does not have use. The concept of time is one that enables us to have a learning vehicle. Each universe, then, is in a particular time if the universe is one of time and space. There are those where this wouldn't necessarily be the case, but they are of worlds very dissimilar to your own.

Let us take an event in time. You have scheduled this gathering next Saturday. Certain preparation is needed for the event. The event is scheduled for 11:00 AM and several beings will be present. Now, how is this affecting you?

"The thought of being prepared is causing me great concern."

So you are living a future moment now?

"Yes."

Each part of your now activity would have injected into it something from the future. This is along the lines of being halfway here or another way would be halfway there. This robs you of part of your energy in the now moment. Now, if something else came along that was scheduled between now and then, even more of your energy would be taken up. Living in the future instead of the present would have as its hazard, stress, wouldn't it?

"I have events scheduled for Wednesday and Thursday, so I started preparations last night for Saturday."

Now, if beings have all of this already in their minds, then other factors can come into play, such as the normal, mundane matters of just living and breathing. These get piled onto your "time schedule" and it is not long until the degree of artificial stress created by the artificial concept of time renders one stressful and inefficient. Ever thought about this?

"I've thought about it a lot and it is not as large a problem as it once was."

How were you able to disconnect it?

"Someone told me to start staying in the now moment."

You are already beginning to see, then, how the effect of time begins to eat away at your concentration in the now moment, rendering you rather incomplete. As has been mentioned, the future is faster than the now and the past is slower. On some level of you, you are in touch with both, but in an area of greater intelligence where this can, in effect, be handled or understood.

If one is artificially in the future, they are artificially attempting to be going faster than the present without the understanding to do so. This results in problems. To attempt to unravel the future without understanding it in the present, or to attempt to be in the future without the knowledge to be there is indeed hazardous to your health. If you imagine yourself in a situation in the future, it would be artifical if you did not have the solution available to solve the imaginary problem. This is where the term "future expectations" would come to bring one into emotional trouble.

Now, we have spoken previously of probable realities, which would then be couched in the term of your future. Now, what I wish to do is to incorporate probable time with these probable realities. It seems that I am speaking of one and the same thing. In essence, they are, but your focus would dictate that some explanation is due. Probable reality and probable time differ only in your viewing port, that is to say, the window or opening through which you bring in energy or knowledge. If your concept of time is one where your view of multi-dimensional reality is fact, then that is one view. If your view is from only the fixed focus, that is another. In other words, probable reality is probably focused differently in each being, depending on his concept of multi-dimensional time.

This is not an easy concept to ingest. Something happened to you and your family but a short while ago to partially explain what takes place. Last Friday, there was a change between you and John. You elected, collectively, to alter your paths. When you changed your paths, you put forth a different field of energy in time and your children picked this up. First, the young one, Danielle, viewed John, with her eyes open in a movie theater, as being completely of white hair and beard in another probable time. Shortly before that, she viewed him with sharper features and of a different personality, younger, but an unknown reality.

Now, your daughter, Mia, in a restaurant, tried to reach you by telephone, in a state of panic. Being older, she viewed you anxiously with, first of all, a pale face and with a negative energy and you shouting in a disparaging way. She could not get hold of you and after discussing it with her friends and continuously trying to reach you by telelphone, brought forth another image of you which was what?

"She saw a vision of me, wearing a pretty turquoise dress, with a smiling face and glowing eyes, sitting in my favorite chair at home."

And what happened next?

"Mia and all her friends imagined a white light surrounding me. They were all afraid I had been killed in an accident or some other horrible event."

Later that night, your son, Johnny, showed up, very frightened that something had happened, but he knew not what. Is that accurate?

"That's exactly what happened."

This appears to be a bizarre coincidence, doesn't it? But, in effect, it probably has something to do with probable time, doesn't it? Now, as time went by, another incident of like kind happened as we were writing this today. (*Seth had just brought forth some amazing information on another probable reality and would then interrupt for a little while.*)

Now, as we continue, you saw Danielle and Johnny call from two separate schools within three minutes of each other, needing to come home, being sick with the same ailments. As you probably could predict, it was but a short delay in time until Mia arrived, not feeling well, either. Now, how could this happen?

Consciousness is multi-level or on many levels at the same time. If one being's time is in time with another being's time, which might be different from your time, then the interaction or connection is made. You

16

might say this would predispose, then, to the same ailment or mode of thinking in time. In other words, time affected them in the same way. At the same time, time would affect you differently. Now, all of these modes of time are available to all, but the choosing is up to each consciousness. You might say that their clocks, run at the same time. Is this clear to you?

"Yes, it is. Last night, John and I resolved the difficulty that was the cause of this whole situation. Today, we have been very happy. But the children all were sick today because their time is different than ours, so, the good change that we are experiencing has not reached their consciousness yet."

It would be in your interest to know that they have decided to use a relatively new method of healing themselves, which prior to this, they were unalterably opposed to.

Your family has been connected or involved over many lifetimes and would then resolve to grow further, hence the telepathic connections which seem to be out-of-the-ordinary. In essence, this sort of thing goes on all of the time in the lives of beings, but unless someone is aware of it, it just does not strike the conscious mind. The ego is something that seeks to have itself proved by "logic." By use of the word "logic" in this context, one could put forth the word "limitation." It would be to your greater edification to stop the use of "proven logic" and open up to the theoretical possibility of other time realities occurring all around you. These realities have a fixed focus in time, as you would view them. Just as there are other probable universes in other probable times and without time, other realities are fixed in their probable phase of time. So, each probable path has a time affixed to it and as it becomes affixed in your consciousness, it becomes your time in actuality. Do you understand this?

"Yes."

If you choose your fixed time of focus, then everyone else changes theirs in relation to yours as evidenced by your children. For instance, have you ever wondered why someone you know would have a sudden change of heart or change of mind? Maybe you have changed your mind regarding them, or letting go, enabling them to change their mind about you. Do you follow this?

"Yes."

There has been a delay of a few months (in time) until the manuscript was started again.

Now, you would find in relation to our last paragraph, that you have evidenced a switch in time "changed mind." Do you know what I mean?

"No."

Do you recall the lady that you were dealing with concerning travel?

"Yes."

What do you think happened there?

"We went to a travel agent to make arrangements for a trip we plan to take. When we arrived, the travel agent was in a bad mood and was extremely cold and rude to us. At some point during the conversation, she switched moods, became very happy and was most helpful to us."

(Seth is rolling around the floor in his chair rather rapidly now, saying, "Just because I've been away in your time, doesn't mean I've gotten out of practice.")

Do you know what happened to the lady?

"No."

After discussing the situation from her "dis-vantage" point, which was one of anger stemming from travail due to her personal relationship, she was treating you as if she was doing you a favor by assisting you. After a short period, you and John wondered why the universe handed you a dis-spirited soul to assist you with this complicated trip. After a few words were exchanged, the lady then changed her mood one-hundred eighty degrees and became extremely helpful and friendly. It appeared that she might have a split mind and you were getting the second half of the split. She became so nice that you found you spent an inordinate amount of time exchanging friendliness.

It would appear that the being then became conscious of another personality in time. Without getting too involved in this, it was a higher vibration of time than the first lady you met in the same body at the same time.

(I just apologized to Seth as I somehow "spaced out" while taking this dictation and he had to repeat the last few words of a sentence. I heard the words he spoke, but suddenly forgot them. I just went blank.)

I guess this illustrates what I was discussing about time, doesn't it?

"Did I slip into another time while you were talking."

Why, that is exactly correct. And so did the lady. If you, with your vibration, in a let us say, Christly plane, put out this higher vibration and it follows divine order, then you will find that all others in the surrounding twenty feet, approximately, sphere will fall into this same, higher vibration. This is the teaching of many adepts and it proves itself by those two examples. Do you understand this?

"No. This is embarassing."

In a way that you are currently learning, you will find that harmony pervades the higher dimension or plane and the use of this plane will circumvent the lower plane. Teachings have been offered for eons attempting to explain this apparent phenomena. Some have offered this as the law of positive thinking. You even have a friend who states, "I AM The Positive Pole Of Polarity." Do you know what this does?

"Yes, saying this with feeling switches me to the opposite pole of wherever I'm at when I say it."

To clarify this, one would use this seeking to switch from negativity to a positive aspect of being. The lady in question, then, by your diligent concentration on your guidance (who suggested you go to this place) caused you to stick to principal (truth) and caused a change of time (mind). Now, from all indications, you still don't quite follow me.

"No, I don't."

If you run into some opposition to your higher intuition, if you do not proceed from a flat form of judgement, then all opposition will be removed by a change in time. This is not easy for beings residing by a clock to understand. This does not appear logical to the fixed mind. What one does here is change one's mind by changing one's concept of time to incorporate time on a higher plane or in effect, no time at all. Do you see why it is necessary to explain by using your personal story?

"Yes, it makes it easier to understand."

For reasons I cannot explain, it is the only way that one could understand, for stories are transitional.

"Every time I tell a story about myself, I actually tell at least five stories, each one understood by the person hearing the story, at the level they are on when they are hearing it."

Now, do you know I could tell you a gray story or an orange story, a blue story or a golden story?

"What?"

What is a blue story?

"A peaceful story?"

From all indications, from your history, it could be melancholy. Is it light blue or is it dark blue?

"Probably shady blue."

Yes, that's a good answer. Depending on its hue, the blue vibration could be melancholy or peaceful. Other colors such as red or violet, being opposite ends of the spectrum, have a corresponding effect upon the receiver, that is, red being somewhat energetic and violet being assuaging. When someone is called a colorful character, you might assume that part of the verbiage relates to his story telling.

Now, a problem would develop using time from past events in the present moment or future. This attempts to stretch the imagination to a discordant point seeking to mix two vibrations relatively different in degree and having them come forth in harmony. This impossible situation is like trying to mix the ingredients for a cake from a spaghetti recipe. Do you know what I mean?

"Yes, I think I do."

Yes, each now moment is different. Yes, reading your thought, I see that you do know.

All right then, why do you think you live where you do in time?

"Because the area provides the situations and energy I need to learn and grow in at this moment."

Good answer, but more specifically, what I wished to ask was why you live here on the West Coast versus the middle of the country or back East?

"What do you mean?"

I mean there are certain qualities to time here, for example, seasonal time, that are different than those

21

in other areas. Specifically, at this latitude with this influence, light will bend at a correspondingly different angle than at other places in your country. The angular velocity of light will reflect differently here in California than in Minnesota, for instance. Your experience, then, would dictate you experiencing this variety of light reflecting the seasons as they are here. For instance, winter and spring are relatively mild compared to other parts of the country. Being in northern California gives you a different variety of seasons than southern California, reflecting hues of your moods in your reflector. Your system needs activation within this harmonic of time which reflects the general vibration of your surrounding geography accordingly. You could say it is within your time frame, but not limited to any given line such as Mountain Time or Pacific Time. Hues of time are reflected within the sphere and greater sphere of influence of your surrounding geography. Since I have never mentioned greater sphere, it would then expand in greater and greater circles to the power of two. It is meant to be a harmonic configuration. A way of understanding is the concept of a pebble dropped in a pond with ever widening circles. Correspondingly then, time is merely an attempt to measure the varying degrees of interception of body consciousness and harmony, which is intersecting angles to circles. Time is angular in velocity, timelessness is circular. In essence, you are speaking of limited and unlimited, but that will do for now.

Not wishing to get carried away, each vehicle (body) seeks to gain experience for the recorder cell of the soul in specific locations which are limited in time/ space until such time as the intersections are no longer needed. That is to say, there is plenty of time.

22

Now, again, you living here would experience a certain quality of time as formed by light rays mixing with your consciousness, forming you and calling it time.

If you continue cosmogony, you will find that there are succeeding intersections upon intersections or universes within universes until infinity is reached. Since most of these are in harmony, seeking to arrange harmony with your intersection of time/space is best served by your current residence or I'm sure you would change it.

What season is it, or should I say what expanded time is it?

"It's fall."

Fall merely means that light from the sun is less intense than in summer, which would allow the formation of greater water density, changing your greater mood or rainfall. Play the words carefully and see how they weigh.

"What?"

Why is it rainfall, not rainsummer?

"Oh!"

Then you could have winter-storm which would be grayer than a summer-storm which probably has lightning. Have you ever thought about this?

"Not really."

All things are arranged in perfect order. You have a composer friend who composed some pale green music that you played when you drove down the road yesterday. What happened all around you when you played this on your magnetic tape recorder?

"A lot of pale green cars appeared around us as we drove."

Was that coincidence?

"No, not at all."

23

Would you say this was a time/space intersection or a "time warp"?

"Is there a difference between the two?"

No.

In a former book, I explained about using old solutions for new problems, that is, taking memories from the past and applying them to the present, resulting in time/space confusion. I only bring this forth presently to explain by example how these intersections take place and apply solutions in the now moment to the now moment. I hope to eventually convince you that all solutions are brought forth without benefit of time, or maybe I should say without hindrance of time.

To avoid the hindrance of past interference residing in the storage battery of the subconscious from falsely influencing the present, one need *"let go of all past time referenced regarding the present now moment."* When one succeeds in letting go of past influence in the present moment, one creates in harmony by not using disharmony, resulting in surrounding oneself with green cars when the color is needed or gray stories when transition is needed or warm blue skies when fresh air is needed. In other words, there is a certain harmony within time which isn't really time, that goes on all of the time, that beings believe they don't have time for. (That would be called a Sethism.)

When I have often mentioned that this book is already written, you believed it was written in time. Isn't that so?

"Yes."

That is not what I mean, of course. I see the finished product, but you in time have to watch it unfold and live it. Does that make you livid?

"Sometimes."

If you don't live it, then you would not have a probable future and you would be out of time and you would be livid.

Nearly every sensation, that is, sight, touch, smell, etc., has the effect of shortening or increasing time in ways I hope to clarify to you. Each stimulus, be it light, heat or any sensation, correspondingly is ordered by you and stored subconsciously, warped by a degree of time. In ways I will try to reveal, one overcomes time by not accepting past or future and has the point of light as the only point of reference.

THREE

FACTORS OF TIME

Time is composed of two separate factors, as beings would understand. The first, which is the major issue of concern, is related to clocks, as has been intimated previously. Since the invention of clocks, the watching or viewing of them has become a preoccupation of mankind. There are many stories of beings racing against the clock and from one standing back in another state of consciousness, it would be humorous indeed, seeing an individual racing against an illusory factor that he has set up to control himself. The setting of such artificial controls is eventually taken in stride by the average individual until such time that the body parts begin to wear out. The body parts wear out due to the artificial time constraints placed upon them by an unforgiving consciousness. The unsuspecting one believes that this is the way to happiness and success.

It need be observed here that the unsuspecting one, as viewed from the higher consciousness, is locked into a geometric block or room that could be classified as prison. It is not viewed in this way because one has brought forth a reflected society as support to keep one's attention into this scene. Mind you now, I am not suggesting that the concept of hard work is not of good purpose. What I am suggesting is that one's artificial constraints due to an artificial time factor will set up one as a prisoner to emotion.

"Wait."

(Whew. Seth forgot that I haven't typed for awhile and I am in time. We've been going so fast that I need a little rest.)

Did you think this was a set up?

"I thought you forgot about me trying to keep up with you on this typewriter."

Is this what is going on with beings in general, do you think?

"Trying to move too fast?"

I guess you got the point, didn't you?

"Yes."

As you know, when you write these books, you live them. That's the rule. How many times do you think this happens with beings in an office, in a factory, or other place of work?

"It happens a lot."

You certainly are taking a lot of time for your answers. What is going on here?

"That is what I'd like to know. What's going on here?"

There is nothing like the present to illustrate a point in the past or future.

"What do you mean? Excuse me, the timer on the stove just went off and I have to take my pie out."

Oh.

"All right, now you have ten more minutes till it goes off again."

That's what I like, being under time and pressure. I believe that's why I left this place to begin with. What I can't figure out is, being out of time and space, I am involved in time and space. This is strange indeed. What is the matter with you? Why don't you type faster? Do you think we have all day? After all, you only gave me ten more minutes. It is a good thing I am not your boss or we would have to dock your pay.

28

Now, you can see how little sense this makes. Everyone knows that in matters of spirit, you do not need to be involved with time and space. But when you try to join the two, there is the potential for trouble. Even with this illustration, it would seem preponderant upon us to come up with a better system. Are your fingernails smoking or is that your cigarette? You know you don't have time to smoke.

"Stop!"

I was just really getting going and now you tell me to stop. How can you deal with this time/space fallacy?

"Will you slow down? I just broke a fingernail and am making too many errors because I can't keep this pace up!"

You're still typing? I stopped talking five minutes ago. What is wrong with you?

"I need a break!"

Oh well, must be some peculiarity of time/space that I don't understand.

"There goes the buzzer again."

Oh, my God. This could be a habit. What next? You can see that the foregoing few minutes, even approaching humor, serves to illustrate that this time/space factor leaves much to be desired. Can one be eternally happy at such a pace? Picture some great adept somewhere, such as Jesus the Christ, racing to take his pie out of the oven or to put a transmission back in a car, racing against the clock. Or, "I have to buy these 'securities' now or I forever will miss the opportunity." Does this seem like a good system to you?

"No, it's too stressful."

Then why do you do it?

"Set up again!"

29

Probably because you never thought about it. Yes?
"Yes."

Few do. Perhaps a better system is to use a unit concept. This would be putting work as unit factors devoid of time. So many units of work would need be accomplished. On good days, that is, those days with no time/space stress, one could accomplish many units, kind of like cubits of time. On other days, when one was emotionally strained, attempting to put out too many units, one might be not what you would call so productive. So then the units become relative units. In such a system, one could be putting forth units of time per month, equating this as production units.

I can illustrate by this example. All That Is comes forth and says, "Seth, I want this book out by February of next year or, Seth, I want this book out by the helical rising of the star, Sirius. It can be done all at once or over time/space. It matters not. Between here and there, the choice is yours." Now, if you were Seth, how would you react to this?

"I don't know how I would react to this."

You are in the same category as all other beings. Not knowing how to let go and let the greater self take over and run the show, one seeks to create artificial time/space boundaries to have a viable system in which to function. What is not known is that a more perfect system already exists. Do you know what that is?

"No."

I know it is tough to admit this, however, many ancient civilizations functioned quite well without the aid of a time piece. Do you know how they did this?

"No."

They had a system within them that enabled them to perfectly attune themselves with their environment so that they could function. Maybe you could call this biological rhythm. I would call it being aware of how to tune yourself to the cycles of All That Is. Did you know that without time pressure you could accomplish more?

"Yes."

How's that?

"I just experienced this as I tried to keep up with you when you were dictating at a rapid pace and I made many typographical errors which will take a long time to correct."

This sounds like heresy. You slow down so that we can go faster. That sounds the opposite from what is taught. That is, it need be speed with accuracy. What you are telling me appears to make sense to me but not to many beings, with the exception of the errors. Now, I know another being who allows these cycles to become attuned in the ancient way, living in this modern world, and appears to be more efficient than others. Efficiency as is measured by production. Do you suppose slowing down and letting go have something in common?

"Yes. When I let go, I slow down and get more done faster."

It might seem I am belaboring the point, but there is something hidden here that normally would defy description in the physical world. Slipping through the cracks is an ancient concept that once again can make its presence known to those who seek higher energy.

Hidden meaning is implied while sifting through the aforementioned string of words. Do you know what I mean?

"Do you mean that the wording in the last few paragraphs will get this point across to us subconsciously?"

In between the ticks of the clock is a space much wider than the conception of time. The effect of the

31

pendulum comes into play to mark the stanza of the advance of space.

This is my first attempt to advance the view of timelessness slipping between the cracks of time. It would go as tick, space, tock. That is, tick, timelessness, tock. Again, tick, infinity, tock. What is missing here? The circle of the pendulum. Do you know what I mean?

"No."

All right. When a pendulum in what is affectionately known as a grandfather clock swings back and forth, that is a tick and a tock. That is a two dimensional swing in a straight line with an arc at the bottom. Between tick and tock, as we mentioned, is a gap. But if you extend tick and tock to a circular concept, that is, squaring the circle, one really has a circular pendulum. Many beings already use pendulums as they might use runes to assist them making decisions. Now, this may not be too easy to grasp. When you have tick and a 180° arc to tock, then you have half of a cycle.

"Is tick one end of the swing and tock the other end?"

Tick is the starting point at 0° and tock is a point of rest before the swing back to tick. There may be considerable argument with my alteration of scientific principle here, but I am not speaking of laws wholly in this plane. So, if beings can allow me discretion long enough to finish this explanation, I will get on with it. What beings sometimes do is to entertain the ego, stating "I know this is incorrect. I learned it in college." I only wish to point out that timelessness is not taught in college. Now, after my digression, do you have understanding so far?

"Yes."

If you then have half a sign wave, you might say that you have half of a bowl equating a circle to a pendulum arc. The equation would have the effect of squaring the circle to the tune of one-fifth of it or 72°. Are you still on my wave length?

"Are you saying one-fifth of a circle is 72° and what does squaring the circle mean?"

That is taking time and corresponding it to time-lessness or infinity. Can you handle that?

"Sorry I asked."

What I have done here is equated a sign wave to a circle to one-fifth and to a square or a fixed dimension. Now, this isn't easy. As I have stated many times previously, probably the most difficult thing of all for beings to grasp is the thought of no time at all. Time really is a series of fixed boxes of emotion or illusion constructed by minds separated from infinity or All That Is. The concept of the unknowable or All That Is was so devastating to beings when the light was lowered by the change in the position of the earth that a new, false concept was devised and has become kind of a religion. What does this mean to you?

(Seth comes back after a brief interlude during which I tried to think of a fairly intelligent answer to this question.)

"What I think you're saying is that when the light was lowered and people forgot who they were, which was part of The All, they created these little boxes of time structure and tried to fill them with things they thought were important to give themselves some feeling of purpose."

Do you suppose I've tricked you a bit?

"Oh, I wouldn't be surprised. Are you telling me that all that effort I put out to answer you was wasted?"

No, I am not. What I am telling you is giving you a key to understanding why there is such a thing as time. There would be no point in going on and on in a more involved fashion when the limited mind would run out of dock space and the boat is going out into the ocean. I have explained a concept of timelessness, but so far, it is not intelligible to you. Do you think every other being who reads this will understand?

"I don't know. This takes a little thought."

But you have brought up a good point. And what was that?

"We're living in the tick and the tock which is the smallest part of the whole pendulum swing. So, relatively, our consciousness is only a minute part of what is going on. What about the concept that when the pendulum stops, before it changes direction, it is going at infinite speed?"

That is a good concept for understanding, but it is not the whole picture. The difficulty with this explanation is that beings are not understanding the relative importance of timelessness relative to time. That is to say, you have a point at rest that would imply infinite speed, but what good does that do you if you cannot advance further with it?

"It hasn't done me a lot of good so far."

What I am seeking to explain is the concept of what isn't. If you have a concept which implies that a timing point of light only is at infinite speed, then one is really not in a position to alter one's concept of the infinite any further than this implies.

What I am seeking to advance is a concept of the relative permanency of timelessness and its over-powering influence relative to space/time. My example serves to illustrate that the little, tiny, fixed points of the tick and tock are *so* minuscule to render infinitely small relative to The All, but still a viable part of The All. The rest of the swing of the pendulum would imply a vast area, indeed, or timelessness. What I am also suggesting by my example is the interconnecting of the various planes of reality making this dimension part of The All. Do you follow me?

"Yes."

The factors, then, that you connect to time are relative emotion only. If you look at a clock, you look at emotion and could as well say, "I will now undergo five minutes of impatience or five minutes not connected with the universe." You could further state during this five minutes, "I will slip into something comfortable such as anger, judgement, hate, depression or some other thought form that would be of limited duration. Thought forms then are what makes time. What does it mean to you when I bring up "Time heals all wounds"?

"It used to mean that if I had a bad experience or felt a loss, I would recover over a long enough length of time. I would slowly get over it. It means something different to me now. My understanding is that all wounds happen in time and that out of time, there is no pain, stress or loss. So, less time not more time would be the healer."

You have this right, however the influence of time is a problem with your explanation. Wounds equal time. If there is no wound, there is no time or conversely, if there is no time, there is no wound. The concept of the timeless dimension is one of no human emotion and one that just is or a state of being. It is not a state of undergoing.

"That's what I just told you. There's high time and low time."

Yes and there are high lives and low lives. Another way of putting the same thing is equating it to light. There are highlights and low lights, which is putting light on the subject.

As an aside, beings will find out that the relative, fixed speed of light now attested as being sacrosanct will, as in ancient times, be found not as fixed as one might believe. This concept is also related to time/space.

As with another book, I implied speed with thought and could go further and imply greater speed or none at all with pictures. Stories tell all form. Most of the great adepts use stories to convey the unimaginable. Somehow, if it could happen to another, it could happen to you.

Getting back to the adage of time and wounds, the duration of the wound as measured in time would be the degree necessary to bury or put out the feeling of the stress that was taken in.

Let us take a being that you might call a cave person. The stresses that a cave person might undergo would be traumatic, indeed, for today's standards. The attack of a wild animal, let us say a saber-toothed tiger, would be so dramatic that it would probably take years off of one of these beings' lives. That is, the emotional stress would be so strong and the connection with infinity so weak that the stress would be difficult to overcome and the shock would have the effect of wearing the body out. In relative years of time, one of these beings might live twenty some odd years comparing it to today's standard of some seventy plus years.

What is not commonly believed, as consciousness expands and the attachment to emotion is released, one does not have to undergo so much time and is then of higher consciousness relative to All That Is. If one has this higher consciousness, then time does not intersect with the body or ego consciousness and one is relatively free from all wounds. Wounds, of course, also include disease. In addition, a being of such a nature could be classified as an adept and would be found ageless. Now, it would be difficult to make such an ointment, as you can see. The fountain of youth is to be found inside of you by lack of emotion.

Getting back to the cave being. With the foregoing explanation, you can see why it would be necessary to come back time and time again to heal enough wounds to extend the life force long enough to eventually interconnect with the Christ Self or the Golden Self so that one could become One. Do you know what I mean?

"Yes."

If you equated this further, you could see that the concept of time relative to lifetimes would soon become meaningless. For instance, one cave person might quickly learn methods of avoiding saber-toothed tigers, live longer and have a more stress free, extended lifetime. The next time in the next lifetime, it would be relatively less stressful and of a higher consciousness and probably in a more advanced civilization.

"Yes, each time he does a little better."

Sometimes he doesn't and would repeat the experience in different lifetimes until it is overcome.

Getting back to this world as you know it, you can see that it might not be so important for growth to accumulate material possessions if it causes one to extend their time unloading karma or emotion that would accumulate along with it. Now, these don't necessarily have to go hand in hand. As each being is different, you can see that the concept of time over lifetimes is really meaningless. Again, you have all of the time you need. It would be to follow one's higher self by following one's interests. Beings incarnating now have certain interests and would pick this time to assist themselves out of this time so they would not be trapped in time by time. Do you know what I mean?

"Yes, I'm one of the ones you're speaking of."

Time, then, can be either extended or rescinded in each now moment depending on one's needs for growth.

37

F O U R

AWARENESS OF
TIME

Are you aware of time?

"Yes, unfortunately."

What time is it?

"About 5:30 PM."

What does that mean to you?

"That means I want to go out to dinner and a movie about now."

Who said?

"By coincidence, I happened to glance at the clock just before you asked the question, saw the time and realized it is time to go out. The clock said so."

Coincidence? Does this mean that there are two incidents going on simultaneously? If this is the case, what is the other one?

"What other one?"

You said, "By coincidence, I looked at the clock and it was 5:30," which would imply that there was another incident going along with the looking at the clock. If this was what you meant, I completely agree with you.

"The other incident was that you asked me the time seconds after I became aware of the time by glancing at the clock, which you didn't see me do."

I didn't?

"No, you couldn't have because I was behind you when I looked at the clock."

Then, how did I know when to ask you about the time? Do you think I'm uni-directional?

"I think that you arranged for the phone to ring so that I would walk over to answer it, walk by the clock and notice the time on the way back to the typewriter which was just prior to you asking the question. I know you're tricky."

Do you know that arrangement was made out of time and it merely intersected with time?

"Of course I knew that."

Would you say I intersected with your probable future?

"Yes."

This brings up a very interesting subject. Do you know that you have some lights which were put together by a friend of yours that cause you and your children to intersect with the probable future prior to it happening? In other words, if I can do this, you can do this. Or, another way to put this, if my oneness can do this, your oneness can do this. Your several lights are really one light. Do you understand?

"No."

By looking at that arrangement of lights, it causes your oneness screen to reflect the probable future. What do I mean by oneness?

"Timeless."

Now, I coached you with that, I will have to admit. However, it is interesting that the probable future is reflected in the oneness. Oneness is a series of vibrations in harmony that coalesce through all octaves. If you get one octave, then others reflect, also. Those lights, then, put together by your mysterious friend, facilitate to a degree that intention. Have you not found it strange that your children think a thought and then it is happening in the probable future?

"Around here nothing is strange."

Well, what is taking place, then, is the lights cause one to project an image into oneness that causes it to be displayed on a screen that is read in the higher mental state of the projector.

It need be explained here that the reason these lights work for anyone is that there is sufficient consciousness to allow one to be receptive to the waves of the probable future. Now, I am calling it probable future, but in the reflector, it really isn't probable at all, is it? In addition, these lights are not controllable, that is, their action by the lower mind would but engage the higher, timeless mind. In other words, they would engage what is called God Purpose of GOP, Good Orderly Purpose. I am told beings like acronyms, so this would be a Sethonym. So, GOP to you.

It seems interesting at this time to bring forth this concept to allow beings to see that there is more going on than the limited ego self would allow one to normally see. What goes on is not written or spoken of except to call it coincidence. After all of that, do you understand why the phone rings when I show up?

"Yes, I do."

(There has been a delay of about a month since we have worked on the book.)

You might say that my timelessness has again intersected with your space at this precise angle. When I couched the term, timelessness, into this parlance, it would imply that I have removed one aspect of the physical world. If I took away your concept of a clock and left you with space, how would you feel?

41

"I don't know. I never thought about it."

Most beings have not thought about such a thing and even the best of you, in reference to these terms, only seek to balance a mythical equation between the two. That is to say, you have some combination of faster or slower time and faster or slower speed between points.

Now, there is a little trick that you have played upon yourself. This trick would tell you that you have placed yourself within the framework of a never ending beat of a stop watch or a pendulum of a grandfather clock. Now, what would happen if I told you, as I suggested in my last book, to change your mood from one of depression to one of happiness?

"Well, I would be happy to have you do that since I am depressed right now."

What seems to be governing this mood?

"There's no particular reason. I just feel depressed."

Does John get depressed anymore?

"No."

Why not.

"It might be because of the program he follows every morning."*

Good guess.

"My second guess is that he's operating in a different time."

What does that mean?

"He's in a higher, faster vibration where the pendulum does not swing so far."

---

*John views a combination of colored pictures, using a variety of colors, including gold and purple, while reciting certain energetic channeled chants until he feels the intersection of energy inside his cranium lift him to a higher vibration. If the reader is interested in these techniques, respond to the publisher and with sufficient demand, we will find a way to share them with you.

How did that happen?

"I guess he just got lucky. Or maybe he meditated his way into this higher state of being."

Another good guess.

"Or maybe it's from being around me all the time. Ho, ho, ho."

I thought you were depressed.

"I was."

Depression, as well as many other emotions, is merely a state called time. In the case of John, he has listened to a number of teachers and has applied what has been taught. One of the problems causing depression is sleep disorder. If beings are out of tune with their harmonic rhythms, they will believe that they are coexisting at a lower state of vibration than they actually are. There is a false sense of difference between what you would regard as past and future, warping one's consciousness into disharmony.

Since I already know I've lost you and probably most readers, I will endeavor to explain. With this emotion, one need change the disorder. John cut his sleep back upon advice, to five to six hours per night with certain program suggestions that are available to everyone. By exchanging the time formerly programmed in the consciousness for sleep, that is a proportion of it, John exchanged conscious thought or living, which was nearer to the now moment. If you told most beings to cut down on the amount of hours they sleep, they would rebel. However, with a small bit of willingness to try something new, they would find their consciousness raised in proportion to that given up, within limits, of course. I do not mean to convey that all sleep need be given up, but if it were reduced to around five hours with an hour for meditation, beings would find themselves, after a regular dose of this, starting to eliminate time/space warp or neurosis. The time spent delving into animal consciousness in extended sleep tends to regress individuals into needing additional "time" in this incarnation to live out what you might call additional karma. It is implied that the preoccupation with sleep in this country is the effect of depression. You could say depression causes sleep and sleep turns depression into a vicious cycle.

If beings really wished to terminate such a cycle, they would reduce their sleep to the threshold where the depression disappears. Do you follow me?

"Perfectly. As you were speaking, I remembered the terrible dreams I had last night and how hard it was to get over the effects of them when I woke up this morning."

The false concept of programming sleep into "hours" is one causing inate confusion to most beings with sleep disorder.

Now, we could say we need so many units of sleep and units of sleep could be measured with a factor comparing them to a factor of heat as measured by your utilities with natural gas. A unit of sleep could be measured as one of quality, not necessarily quantity. Some of the most efficient of beings are those who periodically shut their eyes for a few brief moments, leaning backward with their hands folded behind their heads. You might say that this is opening up your heart out of time. Do you understand this?

"Yes, I've been doing this lately and it makes me feel good."

Birds do it and humans would feel better doing it.

At this juncture, you probably realize that I have been hinting at another aspect of consciousness that is with you but not related to time at all. The concept of time is mankind's attempt to create order out of supposed chaos. But as it turns out, the concept of

44

time creates chaos out of order. Again, seeking to place emotion into a clock only serves to create artificial pressure upon individuals who are seeking to cram emotion into disorienting units called hours, minutes and seconds.

Now, happily there are systems already in creation that when understood will cause beings to beat to the tune of a different drummer. If I give you an angle of 57°, what does it mean to you?

"It means light hits me at that angle."

What does it mean to you if it strikes you at that angle?

"It means that I can hear and understand information best at that angle. My guesses are pretty good, aren't they?"

Yes. Now, how would you equate this to a clock?

"There has to be some mathematical conversion. At 3:00 PM, I can't hear you as well as I can at 8:00 PM."

But it's 3:12 PM, so you can hear me now. *(Seth steps outside and starts playing basketball. He certainly isn't concerned with time today.)*

Now, the sun strikes you and the earth plane at some angle at 8:00 AM and at another angle at 3:00 PM at the same latitude. Depending on a number of factors such as cloudiness and other alignments, the structure or angle of your vibration is governed. What if I told you next Tuesday at 3:00 PM, it will be sunny? What would you say?

"I would say that's great because I enjoy sunny days and I wonder how you know future weather."

So, if I align myself with the right angle, or should I say number on the "telephone", then the future is now.

"What do you mean?"

With the right numerical harmony, which incorporates vibration, one would have a locking key synchronicity that opens the doors to the tunnel that would bring the inverted telescope of the probable future into view. What I am speaking of here is a geometrical configuration of the minds that unlocks the door to the probable future. Each unit of time would have a pre-existing entrance and exit. Each pre-existing (to you) geometric configuration of the stars is angled in such a way that corresponds to your higher mind geometrically that is the key to the time/space intersection. By using a series of simple keys that I will endeavor to convey to you throughout this book, the higher mind could extrapolate the angles through probable time relegating fact on a plane that would show on your conscious screen that the sun would shine at 3:00 PM tomorrow. I will only go a little further at this time and convey that certain angles corresponding to you are time/space tunnels to the cosmos that cause your harmonic resonation with existing geometry circumventing this dimension. Now, I am certain that you understand every bit of this, don't you?

"If I don't, I won't admit it. So, we have to unblock those tunnels, don't we?"

The blockage of these with emotion would alter the angles to what you call the higher planes of consciousness, resulting in ever-widening circles of time.

"I need to ask a question. What about the amount of sleep needed by children?"

The amount of sleep needed by children and all others is directly proportional to the amount of interest or "connectedness" that they have with their greater being. For instance, if a child musical prodigy is practicing his consuming interest, the need for sleep would diminish in direct proportion to the interest. If, on the other hand, someone, including a child, is indolent and listless, then their need for sleep would increase relative to other beings.

"How do you get children interested?"

A good way is to find an interest of the child, any interest, and fan the flames until there is, in effect, a nuclear reaction and the child ignites his own path. For instance, if a child was interested in the flute, like your daughter, and a sufficient geometrical cavity was created for her, she would fill the void with interest until it was what you would call self-perpetuating or self resonating or how to spare the child and spoil the rod. Any other questions?

"Yes. Where do you start?"

Good question. Try the flute with your child just before bedtime and see what happens.

I have mentioned that animals are on this dimension now to serve certain examples for beings to learn. Watch how your cat reacts to certain situations that you would not be certain about. How does your cat eat, for instance? Does she have three square meals per day?

"No. She has about six triangular meals per day."

If you have a triangular bowl, I don't see it on this plane. Now, Muffy (our cat) decides to eat when her biorhythmic clock corresponds to her environment. You might decide to eat something along those lines, but usually would skip one of your segments of hunger causing imbalance in your system periodically. Doing this would throw you out of harmony with other parts of yourself causing your biochemical mechanism to fill the void with energy needed elsewhere, robbing or warping your concept of time. Now, when you avoid your biorhythmic chemical needs, you construct a lower, slower period of time resulting in error and inefficiency, bringing forth frustration and lower emotion, resulting toward time warp and sleep. Telling you this would be disconcerting to you and others like you, however, it is only by self-induced change that you would attempt conversion of your anti-biorhythmic time extension into a happier, more efficient state.

"What is self-induced change?"

When you realize that you are deficient with your thinking regarding food, you would induce change by programming your sleep and meditative states using your greater self to bring forth a timeless method for rearranging your thought pattern. Periodically, beings introduce their emotional cycles from their lower stratum such as "lighting a fuse" and watching the explosion occur. Self-induced program changes will pull the fuse when it is realized that it has been ignited, prior to it overflowing all of the registers of your computer.

Beings develop habits, good or bad to their judgment, which are programmed into their subconsciousness early in life resulting in nearly automatic behavior. When they inject themselves with a dose of programmed behavior, usually the cycle runs on until an artificial clock stops it, such as the end of the work day or until the registers are burnt out (tiredness).

A more efficient way to break up these patterns which extend and overlap the clock would be to induce periodic states of consciously looking off into the distance or closing the eyes temporarily with the hands clasped behind the head as mentioned before. This has the tendency to bring one into the now moment away from rote, unconscious behavior. The now moment is not in time and therefore does not consume energy, either. By breaking up these automatic cycle patterns (psycho patterns), you constantly would refresh yourself along your path no matter what you are doing. You can do and be coincidentally. Do you follow me?

"Yes."

Oh! Tell me how you do and be together.

"Caught."

Now, I was watching you as you were typing and I saw that you were in your rote register. And I knew that I if asked you the question, you would just agree with me so that you could continue your program. The reader might stop at this point and ask himself the question, "Am I into rote reading behavior?" In other words, "Am I in my automatic mode?" Then you would ask, "What time is it?" Or, "What hollow in space am I filling which is not connected to all other space?" When you realize that your space is not connected to all other space, then you must be in time.

F I V E

SPEED OF TIME

Over some time, there has been the thought that light travels at the rate of approximately 186,000 miles per second and that this would have some correspondence to something that you call time, which corresponds to something called space. Now, I know of this being from another plane of reality who is capable of manifesting physically here, who would say that this is in error and based upon measurements that were erroneous to begin with and is only relative at best if you categorize the speed at approximately 182,000 miles per second. The travel of electrons through a measured wire or circuit also corresponds to this number and is an apparent limitation to modern technology.

As an interesting aside to this, we also know this "bodyless being" who has suggested that if you built an optical telescope four times larger than the largest currently known on the earth plane, you would really extend your vision into time, but would accomplish nothing.

Another way of looking at the same equation would be to enlarge existing technology independently of higher "harmonics" and continue to complexify time, further extending it and confusing the minds studying this if it is not tied to something called higher cause. It might appear that I am seeking to degenerate technology, but that is not what I am about. What I am suggesting is that if the scientific community would seek to deny the existence of a higher plane of reality causing the phenomena of time, one would be in a never ending, closed spiral. It would take an intersection from a plane of higher vibration to correspond with the laws of lower harmonics, opening the way to a rejoining of higher harmonics to lower harmonics. Now, what does this have to do with you?

If one was involved with an infinitely increasing series of complexity, one would find himself in a quagmire leading to confusion. If one seeks to apply the higher law to correspond to the lower, one would find energy that could explain any perceived difference. Practically, one would find a correspondence of different phenomena such as emotion that would be far in addition to known law. As Hermeticists have taught over eons, anger in the lower mind corresponds to non-anger or happiness in the higher mind. There is something called vibration which is a real measure of speed, not the clock. Let us take, for example, hate, which is a relatively low vibration in the physical world. How do you feel when you hate,

"I feel terrible when I hate. I lose all my energy."

How does your clock function?

"It slows down. Time drags."

Does the spring in the clock cause the hands to move more slowly?

"No. It's my perception that changes."

So the tick of the clock is merely a mechanical contrivance not related to emotion?

"Yes."

I can only hope to explain how important it is to realize the relative difference between relying on this clock and that of emotion. Further, something such as anger has a distinct vibration and will cause conception of time to go at a different rate than that of, say, jealousy. Now, since each of these emotions and all others have a corresponding rate of vibration, they in turn correspond to rates of vibration of diseases such as cancer, joint strain and swollen glands. Each one of these emotions, if you had a meter sensitive enough to measure it, would vibrate correspondingly with a similar geometric place within your physical body. For instance, anger would correspond with your lymph system through the vegas nerve causing it to raise or lower its balancing system with your body, producing an effect of good health or relatively bad health. Concentration upon a negative thought, judgment, etc. causes a slowing down of the vibration of your body, dragging your consciousness with it to a slower, more sluggish level, forcing it into a state of health that is not conducive to happiness. With this, there is a correspondent transfer of geometry among all systems of the body, adjusting the levels of each organ, gland, etc., to the corresponding vibration of the thought. This is done at or near infinite speed whereby the servomechanism of the body transfers according to your thought hues to the corresponding balance points in your body system. For instance, the thought of a particular, pushy individual may cause your knee to hurt or back to hurt. Some holistic type beings might say that there is too much of a load placed on the physical structure by the mental system. Imagine the stress placed upon the system by the orderly transmission of stimuli, first of all from the five senses and then thoughts, which would add up to thousands during a given waking period. What I mean to imply here is the orderly transmission of stimuli at immeasureable speed, which is a controlling aspect of what you call time. Already, we are in trouble because we have infinity intersecting with time.

As many beings know, looking at the star, Sirius, supposedly the stimuli that you see were transmitted eight years ago to reach you in this time frame. That is to presuppose that there would be no other influences brought to bear. This is saying that there is a static state devoid of higher mind. What actually happens here is a corresponding shift in a pattern of Sirius which greatly influences this planet would instantaneously by transfer through infinite geometry, affect you. One of the greater difficulties with current thought would be to deny this because of a supposed lack of higher mind connection of this transfer at infinite speed by the higher mind. There are many beings who currently are capable of remote seeing, that is, seeing in two places simultaneously, who hesitate to mention this ability for fear of ridicule by accepted political science. It is not my place here to take on the structure, as this is already conditioned by the current geometric alignment which governs the condition. To escape this fixed velocity would be to enjoin the higher mind to order intelligence to the conscious, physical nature.

There are objects on this planet that by their very construction, cause a resonation of geometry with a subject's mind to cause the subject to see in higher dimensions. For instance, going inside any one of the three pyramids at Giza in Egypt or in several other pyramids throughout the earth, one may be spiraled into another state of consciousness that currently cannot be measured in time. The altered state of consciousness, like the dream state, will be devoid of time, causing one to see across a grid system that enjoins the mind to see holographically at right angles.

It has been said by you and others that you see with your ears, hearing being a higher seeing. You already know someone who sees at a ninety degree angle from the direction in which she is looking. For instance, an object on the wall beside her which cannot be seen, with closed eyes is then intuited in the higher mind. Now, you've had issues of this remote seeing, also. Did you not see, ahead of time, a scene from a recent trip?

"I saw various places on the island of Maui the night before our first trip to Maui."

Now, as a satellite views from a high altitude to enable its cameras to photograph weather, so does an aspect of you that we'll call a podule, project itself into a holographic system, enabling you to see Maui with good, orderly purpose. Remember GOP. You would cause electrons in your system to intersect with electrons in anther system to cause a golden mirror to remotely view a distant object. All beings, whether they realize it or not, see their future from a few seconds to some distance ahead of time depending on their ability to let down their gates. You might perceive we are speaking of what you call time/space vortices or wormholes. What happened when you viewed remotely this tube that was nineteen feet six inches long and six inches in diameter with the cross on the end?

"I visualized the tube with the golden cross at the end, imagined my problems spelled out on the cross and let them go."

What color was on the other side of the cross?

"Burnt-orange."

What color was the pyramid mountain by the lake in Canada?

"It was burnt-orange and the leaves on the trees were gold."

What happened then?

55

"We were standing in front of a lake at the foot of the mountain and saw the shadow of the mountain cast a gold cross in the water in front of us. We were amazed."

Did a boat go by at that exact instant?

"Yes, it did."

Was this not prophecied from a coin that appeared by suggestion from a friend of yours?

"Yes, that's what happened."

What do you think happened here?

"The symbolic things we've heard about actually happened to us."

Yes, by use of symbolism, higher geometry was caused to manifest in your physical world ahead of time. How many times has it been that you have seen the same sort of expression? You think of someone and there they are. Someone once said, "I think, therefore I Am." You could say, "I think, therefore you are," or, "You are a result of my coincident thought." You could go on and on with this, but it would appear the point has been made.

Can you measure mind speed?

"No, it's at infinite speed."

There would be instants of this, but at other instants, the well can be clogged with emotion. You are the sum total of your thoughts and if they are blocked with emotion, this acts as a governor to your concept of time. As stated in another book, it is speed of thought or acceleration of divine image. Do you know what I mean?

"No. I hate having to say no."

(Seth gets a piece a paper, draws something on it and holds it up.)

What is this?

"A triangle."

Do you know I can see around corners with this or slow down time?

(Seth walks into another room and comes back with a glass, four-sided pyramid.)

Now, ordinarily you could not see someone around a corner because your vision might be blocked by a building in the way, let us say. So, you could put a mirror at a forty-five degree angle and spot him coming. Now, you could have an additional mirror at another corner of the building at forty-five degrees and literally see someone who is approaching on the other side of the building "through the building."

So, do you understand me?

"Yes."

So far, everyone can understand this. Now, let us say that I am a resident of another dimension and I desire to communicate with you. What is the easiest method to use? Well, as it would seem to indicate by using mirrors, one need alter speed to intersect with you from the other dimension. Now, when I held up this triangle, how long did it take you to recognize it as a triangle?

"I don't know."

You could be clever and say, "I recognized it at the speed of light," but then I would merely take it around the corner and draw another figure on the paper and if you and I so desired, you would be able to recognize it without seeing it with your physical eyes. At this point, you would be seeing it in the now instant or now moment. Why do you think that you might see it faster remotely than you would with the physical eyes? Since it is impossible for you to answer this, I will explain. You have lower conciousness which is indicative of physical seeing. You then have higher consciousness which one might term remote seeing, although I would quarrel with this term. The truth of the matter is you see the object no matter where it is at infinite speed and it is only the limitations placed upon your seeing by your consciousness that would slow down your viewing. Do you understand this?

"I've experienced this, but I don't understand it."

Well, we seem to have a problem here because we have apparently alternative lines of force. That is to say that there would be an apparent distinction between the lower and higher consciousness at or near the speed of light. Nothing is further from the truth and it is only false reference to a concept called logic that would seek to again denote the artificial time lines. In essence, they do not exist and would only be the result of false perception making them appear real. One gets vague references to something called optical illusion. This is a catch-all phrase attempting to explain a higher law manifesting on the physical plane that is not understood.

Now, with this glass pyramid and the aforementioned illustrations with the buildings and mirrors, what would happen if I had a series of interdimensional upside-down and right-side-up pyramids interlocking on their side faces? I could theoretically have an infinite number of pyramids going out into any direction or into infinity. If I wanted to stack them up, I could then have angles of force bent nearly any direction. There is an old axiom called, "As above, so below." I am happy to report that it still works. As light is bent by this glass pyramid below, what would cause anyone to think that it would not be bent in a similar form with some energy from above that you could not see with your physical eyes?

"Logic. If I can't see it, I can't prove it."

I don't remember setting you up as the devil's advocate, or is it judge advocate? What the higher law generally expresses in the physical plane is first a testing of the water to see if you are receptive, kind of like the carrot and the stick. If you are curious, you may be receptive and pursue the matter further. If you are bound up in logic, you may fail to see the opening and shut the door until next time.

What I am saying is that each being has a divine mirror in a geometrical form conducive to his insight that causes the divine reflection to manifest in his consciousness when he is receptive. All of this takes place already and is in place out of time and space. It is the geometry of your condition.

Already you can see that there might be a slight conceptual problem with the idea of limiting time to a certain speed. When one places limitations logically upon his consciousness, he has the effect of putting a veil over his consciousness, causing extension of time.

Do you remember the odd looking device that John put over his forehead? It had a ruby, an emerald, a crystal and a piece of copper.

"Oh yes, the Sirius Device. He played basketball while wearing it and the accuracy of his shots doubled. It sure surprised our son, Johnny, who was playing with him."

Now, only you and the children saw this, for the neighbors might have thought he was odd, indeed. You must keep a viable persona in your neighborhood. Think what would happen if you were watching professional athletes wearing such a thing. It seems that some of the strange looking crowns from ancient civilizations had uses other than decoration. You might say that this geometry caused a precognitive adjustment in the flight of the ball, enabling it to be controlled on its way to the hoop. Now, I realize this goes against the grain of logic and logicians would hang you at sunset or is it sunrise?

"I believe it's sunrise and we don't have to do that this time around. We were hung in Ireland already in another lifetime."

Yes, that was not one of your better lifetimes as you would view it.

The geometry of the copper gadget would enable the mind to alter by expansion its viewing plane to enable it to more accurately control the ball.

Speed of time, then, is a relative conception of the mind and has little or nothing to do with reality and especially the clock.

The transfer of geometric images that would be unlimited in themselves is accomplished at or near infinite speed. The only restricting influence of the speed of time is one's personal decision to limit it by emotion.

Last night you saw an apparent phenomena whereby the moon appeared to be several times larger and closer than you would view normally. What is normally said about such a phenomena?

"Must be an optical illusion."

In other words, you need a new pair of glasses.

"I don't think so."

The silver crescent at the angle of light reflecting from the sun caused the refraction of light to be recepted by your intuition, enabling you to perceive the moon at a relative distance in your consciousness. Notice this implies that your consciousness receptor would be at a relative different vibration than other beings'. Now, other beings might well indeed perceive the phenomena similar to your viewpoint, but being apparently separate from you, would not appear to view it as your physical eyes would. Did other beings see the moon like this?

"Yes, I talked to a few who did."

So, the moon in its silver-ray mode would apparently be closer than its gold-ray mode. Is that what you mean? Is that what is meant by silver threads among the gold?

Light is bent according to the available geometry and would spread itself in a fashion to cause your consciousness to view it at some level of vibration. So, you could say, "I am seeing the moon relative silver and close tonight", or "I am seeing the moon relatively gold and distant tonight." It seems a matter of vibration might explain this phenomena quite easily. The difference in rate of vibration of the two colors causes you to view the moon further or closer depending on the ray.

CHANGE OF TIME

This is relative Seth. I am relative to you, to your particular vibration in your time/space choosing. Now, you are going to ask me a question.

"As you were speaking, the thought came to mind that I would like to see you with my physical eyes, but I have a mental picture of you already and I know it is not the same as others have because I have seen a picture of you drawn by someone else and it looks nothing like you look to me."

How do I look to you?

"You are going to laugh. You look tall, thin, handsome, thoughtful, humorous, relaxed, a person who does not take anything very seriously."

I'll accept that. I'll put my new picture on the wall. In other words, as you grow, so do I. You might say that I have taken on new stature. It would seem to indicate a change in time or of time. From short, squat or old, to tall, lean and handsome isn't a bad change of time. Next you might even say I had achieved being suave and debonaire.

"Now that you mention it..."

Now, everyone knows I'm holy. I wonder if other entities act this way. I'll have to check the dictionary of entities and see if this is proper behavior. Or is it proper motion?

By our kidding, we have already established a change in time. When you change your mind, you change time and you change space accordingly. I've changed states. You haven't. I like warmer, weather, when my thermostat works correctly, that is. Wouldn't it be funny to see me watching television, sitting there whether it was on or not, for it wouldn't make any difference to me.

Now, overhead currently in what you call your solar/star system, is a clock of a different color. Notice that in the absence of clouds or other conditions, the sky is a pale blue. That is conducive to the transfer of energy where you need it most within your system. Imagine waking up to a black sky or a green one. Somehow, this just would not be conducive to the same old world, would it? So, when you wake up in the morning and see a pale, blue sky, you could say, "This must be earth."

Did you ever feel that you were governed by your moods?

"Yes, all the time."

In other words, if you're in time, you're in mood. How do you describe this concept of time? I see there is doubt on your face, so I take that to mean it is nearly indescribable. Most beings, when asked how their day went, proceed to fill you in on a series of events that you could pretty much time and that is their description of a day that was either good or bad. If you could plot a graph of mood versus how beings feel, you would see one-on-one correspondence between the events described and their relative state of health.

A series of timed events would be something in time that just rolled forward or on in some fashion that most beings would seem to have given the control to some aspect other than themselves. Do you know what I mean?

"I could barely type the last two paragraphs, much less understand them."

(Seth is now across the room, throwing darts.)

Bull's eye! I stuck one dart into another and then caught them both in mid-air.

Now, do you think that my throwing those darts would suddenly change time?

"Probably."

So, as I have mentioned in previous books, I am affecting the probable future by my choice in the now moment. Without such a choice, many beings would take it that time is a series of preprogrammed events with something called work that is beyond their consciousness to change.

At this juncture, I will part ways with these thoughts. The pale, blue sky still contains unseen the influence of astronomical geometry that more closely governs the condition of non-conscious behavior than beings do with their conscious minds. Yesterday you felt a rather peculiar influence that, unseen, appeared to influence many beings. Beings thought that they, themselves, were the somehow mysterious cause of their negative feelings. The unseen sky at that time had an influence on many who did not even have a thought that such a thing was going on. Except for those residing in the sphere of the constellation of Leo, most others were unduly influenced.

Can you imagine someone in an occupation, be it office or outside working, not realizing the significance of this influence, taking it all in stride and just saying, "I am having a bad day." Few would say, "Why am I having a bad day?" Those who would might say, "I didn't sleep well last night. I ate poorly last night." Or, "That being I had words with over my wonderful driving probably upset my whole day. Of course, the boss is in a very bad mood, also. As a matter of fact, everyone around me is in a bad mood. I wish I was in Bermuda."

Have you ever been in this situation?

"A few times, yes. Have you noticed that a lot of my an-swers have the word "time" in them? I think somebody is playing with my brain and mouth."

Are you asking me if you can have some of my time.

"You don't have any to give."

That's true, or space, either.

Let us take, then, the one who finds himself in the unenviable position of having a bad day. This being is probably explaining, "I don't have time for this," while extending time. "Maybe I'll stay overtime tonight to make up the difference for what I couldn't get done in time." At this juncture, it might behoove the unfor-tunate one to stop for a bit and reconsider the time/ space trap that this artificial synthesis has woven. What would you do about a situation like this?

"There are a number of things I do, the most important being the realization that something is off and it may not be me. Then I ask John what stones I should wear to offset any negative energy. I make sure I exercise, eat right, meditate and read something spiritual. I try to use a sense of humor and ride the waves until things change."

(At this time, the phone rings. It is a friend, Corinne, calling to tell me what happened to her while she was medi-tating this morning. She was, holding a crook in one hand and a flail in the other, two ancient Egyptian objects, to aid her meditation. Suddenly, her eyes opened wide and she saw the right side of the room at a 45° angle, the same angle at which the crook in her right hand was held. The left side of the room appeared to her to be at a 45° angle in the opposite direction, the same angle at which she was holding the flail in her left hand. Then her eyes closed and she continued her meditation.)

Probably a mirror coincidence.

(Our daughter, Danielle, just came in from school and told us that tomorrow is Fifties Day at school and asked if I would help her to dress up like people did in the fifties.)

I wonder if this would shorten time or change time. Do you ever wonder at why this continues to happen when we write these books? Do you suppose we've changed time in some way?

"I've wondered about this many times and never figured it out."

The top of the pyramid is where the sides come to a point, is it not?

"Yes."

Five mirrors reflect oneness and the point of light. If you scatter the images of light and have them the spiral focus at a point, you will see where one plane of reality intersects with all others. We would imply, by example, situations to lead one into a knowingness where the intersection of points of light connect. One point of light holograpically interconnects with all other points of light, bringing forth what you would call the Christ Consciousness.

When the worker stood back and sought to change his day, first of all, he needed to be open to a change of mind. If the geometric lenses in the pale, blue sky could be imagined to bring forth a point of light or a pre-existing condition that intersected with his life, a realm of awakening could be entertained.

As I have attempted humorously to imply by my various antics as we write this, so would the worker be helped by a letting go of existing activity and a complete change of mind briefly into another activity. The other activity, in this case I was throwing darts, would have another energy, a fun energy, attached to it with a certain mind set. This removes one from the previous mind set or vibration and causes one to see the moon as a larger object.

"Yes, because you're open."

You might say the new activity, although temporary, is a different room with different colors than the previous activity.

Now, someone might say, "Seth, you cannot play darts in the office or out on the construction site." That is a good argument for darts, but does not preclude one from having a little pocket game that would intensely grab their attention elsewhere or, the room that are in the mind. What is interesting here is that each successful transit into another "room" will enable the pale, blue sky with its geometric hidden star geometry to infuse the worker with new light or energy injecting balance into his conscious receptors.

Each energy center, as I have implied, has certain angular degrees of light. For instance, the area known as your third or Christ Eye would be open and balanced at 45°. A shift away from time allows its geometry to flex into balance, causing renewed energy to the physical structure.

As you implied, you could then pick up a particular stone such as an uncut sapphire for Taurus, holding it in your hand briefly, having it alter your vibration when Taurus is overhead. The problem here is one's mind set that would compel a being to say, "I don't have time to fool with this sort of thing. I am busy and therefore, I don't have time to carry a bag of stones or a silly game. What I am going to do is sit here and continue with this until I get finished, even though I may have a terrific headache." It is only when this being would be so"sick and tired" of the headache or other stress that this being would be maleable enough to try something different, shortening time.

There is a certain "pride" about being able to work fourteen hours with but little break, bragging about how much work one has accomplished. The sad fact is a worker has merely extended his time until he has had enough of the attachment to work and is willing to let go of this concept long enough to alter time. Does this make sense to you?

"Yes."

(Again, a delay of a few days.)

Now, you can see that what I have spoken of has happened to John and several others. There are many ways to put the mind at balance. Your ego is set in a certain way that would need a change periodically to result in harmony between body, mind and spirit. Now, spirit also includes soul in this context. In John's case, he was so intent on various spiritual or mental projects that he forgot about the body aspect. If it was a sunny day, he seemed to be entranced with his project and forgot to sniff the air. One advantage that you have in this area is the air is inherently more sniffable at this juncture of the year than others. When you sniff now, you don't get a snoot full of smog, do you?

"No. Sorry it took me a minute to answer you. I was trying to figure out how to spell 'snoot full.'"

There is a certain harmony or maybe you could say balance to you and your surroundings. If the weather in the winter time happens to "act" springlike, maybe to be in harmony with nature, you would decide to take advantage of some extraordinary weather while it lasted. If you persisted in your mind set, then it might pass you by and you would be out of harmony with your environment. Have you ever done such a thing?

"Yes, many times."

Have you ever considered that your moods were preprogrammed for you without the distraction of time?

"Yes, I think that perhaps all surrounding conditions are created by me to bring about certain learning situations."

What if, as some of your dear friends joke about, you needed to finish this book by a certain time, but the weather was conducive to outdoor activity and further, you decided that it might be in your interest and mine to finish in spite of the attractive weather outside?

"I have a strong feeling we would be late finishing the book."

Do you think this is a preconditioned response?

"I think it's what is happening. We're already late and these little things keep coming up for us to do which keep us from working on the book."

By whose clock, yours or mine? Have you ever noticed in sessions with other beings that they will suddenly start speaking on some subject that is on everyone's mind, including mine?

"Yes, I regard that as coincidence. Just kidding."

Do you suppose that if you had a certain geometrical alignment at a particular, shall we say, time, that certain beings would be there and certain things would be said?

"Yes, I do. That also happens when we write these books. I'm always saying things other than what I think I am going to say."

Do you mean that I am twisting your mind?

"I think so."

Do you suppose those ancient Egyptian beings who had the strange looking hats in odd geometric configurations used them as antennae?

"Why do you ask?"

If you put out or up a certain antenna, you will cause certain ideas or thought to configure resulting in that geometric idea. I guess this is saying thoughts are things, but in a different fashion, so to speak.

"Do you mean that if I wear a pyramid on my head, I will think like a pyramid?"

It is this sort of parallel that I had in mind. Just as on certain days, you wear certain colors and act in certain ways. And on other days, you wear other colors and act differently. What is not immediately recognized is that your physical appearance actually changes vis-a-vis other beings' perception of you.

Now, you have this video tape with a number of your friends in it that keeps changing in time each time you view it. Why do you think this is?

Seth just told me that he thought it was time to change the page I was typing on. As he spoke, I was typing the last word on the last line of the page. Seth could not have seen that as he is sitting across the room, facing the back of the typewriter. Then Seth asked me if I had run out of time or space or place. I guess he proved his point. I also notice that he is dictating much slower than usual today, so he must know that my arm is tired from playing racquetball too long last night and I can't type at my usual speed.)

"To tell you the truth, we've all discussed this phenomena, but I still don't understand why the film changes every time we watch it."

Ever watch an old movie?

"Sometimes."

Does it appear "old" to you?

"Yes."

Is it out of style, out of mind or out of time?

"All of the above."

It's actually out of geometry. There is no longer a harmonic resonance and it is no longer within the scope of your now moment.

What I am saying is that we're not really speaking of space or time in this context. We are really speaking of a state of mind which beings are seeking to wrap around a time clock.

You and John have attempted to alter your life to the degree that you would be at harmony with your environment. Now, this is not taken to mean that you eat certain things, smoke or not smoke certain things or use certain products which would be politically expedient to broadcast. It means that in the most responsible way that you can harmonize with all that becomes your stimulus, you seek to alter your life to make it conducive to this harmony. This is not easy to explain and again, I am attempting in little ways to bring this idea into action by suddenly throwing darts or playing with the cat or talking to your children who may wander through at any given geometry (time). One of the difficulties here is that to connote harmony, we use the word time and then proceed to distort it. For the type of idea I am attempting to get across, there are really no words. One of the reasons that there are no words available is that I am attempting to describe a wordless, timeless, spaceless environment where they would not be necessary. Do you understand me?

"I'm not sure."

Let us go back to the worker that we previously discussed. Does the anger of his boss arrive prior to the worker's action which purportedly caused it? In other words, is there anger out that day?

"There has to be. The boss had a need to vent anger, so he created the worker doing something that would cause him to respond angrily. If it hadn't been the worker, it would have been someone else."

Now, there could be certain alignments, geometrically speaking, of planets and stars and other factors which would pre-create these conditions.

Here again is where probable worlds come into focus. To the degree that you successfully tune yourself to a higher vibration will depend on the probable reaction of your boss. For reasons that would be difficult to discuss at this time, if you are on a higher spiral of vibration, your intersection with your boss would also take place in a different plane of reality than if you were on a lower vibration. You might say that there would be several different stage plays going on concurrently. The stage play by which you interact is governed by your choice of vibrational level.

You could change your current stage play instantly by changing your mind and all other minds that intersected with you would change their minds in proportion to the degree that you have changed yours. Notice I have used the word *degree*. This implies an angular velocity of energy. Now, what in the world does that mean?

"The angle determines the speed."

Good answer. As you determine your course to harmony, you then change your electromagnetic angle producing a faster flow of light through your river.

You have seven wheels that open the eighth gate. To get a conducive or harmonic flow of energy through your system, you need open your gates to the perfect angle that would cause the least resistance. If any one

73

or more of these wheels is not angled properly because of some ego resistance or false resistance, then
there would be an impedence to the flow resulting in
loss of energy and an extension of time.

When you decide that the resistance has heated to
the point that is untenable to you, then you need
change your mind, which in turn would change your
time, which in turn would change your place or space.

It is so difficult to use this language or any language
to convey a message which is not contained in language. When you start speaking, you start slowing
time and the resultant message then becomes prohib-
itively slow. So, now that I'm speaking, I have linearity and you can start setting your clock. Notice I
have used the term "set the clock." I didn't say "flow
the clock."

"How do you flow your clock?"

You flow your clock by letting go of it. Harmony is
not linear.

"I'm thinking about this."

It has taken this much space to get to this point.
Maybe I could say it has taken this much space to get
to this non-point or I could say, it has taken this much
time to get to this non-space. Then someone would
say that this seems to be non-sense. We could really
get carried away with this and start adding syllable
upon syllable to further distort meaning.

What I am seeking to accomplish is to cause the
reader to disconnect *what is* from *what isn't*. There might
be a geometric connection between Monday and rain
and Tuesday and sun, but only in a broad spectrum
encompassing many individualized presences would
the connection become clear. In a narrow sense, indi-
vidually, it probably would not become clear until vi-

brations were raised to the extended plane of a geometric idea.

All things are cause and effect, but part of the casual plane is beyond beings' recognition, especially if they are fixably focused on a particular outcome. It may seem boringly repetitive to repeat that to enclose oneself in a fixed environment without changing your created room would not be conducive to harmony. So again, a change of time is a change of mind.

RELATIVITY

There have been many ideas regarding time and one of the most famous was Albert Einstein's Theory on Relativity. This would be relativity with regard to the speed of light, which was mentioned in a previous chapter. What I propose is to attempt to explain the relative speed of time by inferring to something called the relative mind.

The relative mind is not fixed in time or in any other plane of reality. It is a broadened scope which enables one to alter the frequency (vibration) of this state of mind and alter the scope by this extension, enabling one to envelop or be enveloped by oneness, which goes beyond the physical plane of reality.

It has been said that we are in The Father's meditation and are given our reality by this interchange. Each stimulus, physical, mental or spiritual that interacts with our being causes a proportionate change of mind, altering our frequency of reality. Just as a cosmic particle traveling at nearly infinite speed will alter another slower particle which has already intersected with an aspect of time, so shall the influence of infinite energy as it intersects, or you will allow it to intersect with your being, alter you. You are the altar to be altered. You are the temple of the infinite selection, but I am not speaking of anything associated with Darwin. Just as so-called spores purport to induce change in a fixed environment, energy willed in by higher reality will cause change in the physical environment.

There appears to be a linear progression of civilizations starting at one time and leading to another. Actually, nothing further from the truth is reality. Did the ancient Egyptians, as you know them, suddenly become brilliant? Why does it have to be that they needed to become smarter as time progressed? Actually, they seemed to have been smarter in the beginning and not so smart as time went on. You might say they took nearly non-time and made time out of it. Or maybe another way to put it is they took geometry and created time from it. Can you think what it would be like now without time?

"It would be fun."

How is that?

"There'd be no worry about sleeping a certain number of hours or eating at certain times or working a set number of hours and days or stretching our paychecks a certain number of weeks. We could do what we feel like doing when we feel like doing it."

Theoretically, this seems like an ideal situation. But, what is preventing this?

"Lack of discipline, irresponsibility, guilt for not accomplishing enough."

That's enough. I get the idea. By not being responsible, one would not be responding to the stimulus of the point of white light or another way of putting it is one is out of harmony. Now, it is true to a certain degree that this time/space intersection with geometry is conducive to the application of lessons in materialism. But there is a rapidly approaching change in the focus on the material world. It is not my way to even imply that there would be coming any harmful events to beings. What I am implying instead is a change of the geometrical lens enabling the experiencing mass of humanity to focus in a less timeful fashion.

What might have happened to a civilization such as the ancient Egyptians who suddenly got smart?

"Probably a lot of chaos."

If you mean by chaos, the introduction of knowledge from a higher plane, I would agree.

"That's what I meant."

Now, if you say relativity could mean relative to, let us say, infinity, then you could say you might be open to all possibilities. If this be the case, why couldn't a society such as the ancient Egyptians be suddenly infused by brilliance instilled by a great teacher who happened to arrive from a different plane?

It is widely accepted that the teachings of Jesus the Christ, when Jesus the man, were bringing forth information beyond the scope of most humans. Was Jesus relatively smarter than all other beings or did he have access to higher teachings from an expanded plane? If it was the latter, would he be the only one ever allowed access to such a plane? This is not reality to suppose, even as the great master taught, that he would be the only one with this access.

The ancient Egyptians also had access by divine intervention of such a master who, by imparting this knowledge to the local populace, enabled them by infusion to become a very sophisticated civilization. To try to fit history into a linear scope, as Darwin and others have attempted, is as impossible as trying to place all of the ocean in a thimble.

Mankind's ego has a need to force its supposed reality into a linear sense in spite of the facts. This supposed order, out of chaos, will not stand up or survive factual scrutiny. If mankind could allow the luxury of a non-linear, relative focus, even temporarily, a truthful system of reality would then be presented. Do you have a need for a linear focus?

"A bit."

Can you imagine a world where yesterday and tomorrow, although having different events, would be viewed the same? It would be kind of like a round ocean being hit randomly by rain drops. Do you follow me?

"I am having a little difficulty imagining a world like that."

Take a round space instead of a square one. The wrapping effect has overlapped. In other words, a round space wrapped around a round object has greater attraction to spiral density than a square. If you will bear with me a moment, I will seek to explain. All things are spherical and to try to fit linearity into them has presented the physical world of yours with a seemingly insurmountable problem. Time, as you know it, is a linear unfoldment. Your greater mind works from spherical density. To unravel the greater mind into a linear layout, which is time, would be to warp the image, making it untrue. Look in the mirror. What do you see? Do you see a square or a round image? Have you ever thought about this?

"No, I haven't."

What is a reflection? Is it square image in time or is it a reflection of the sum total of your reflected being? What time is it in the image? You could say "Seth, you can hold your watch up and then you will know what time it is in your image. That's only logical." Then I will counter with, "Look again after five minutes have elapsed upon your clock and tell me if you see the same image." What would you think?

"I don't think there is any time attached to my image in the mirror."

That's the spirit, so to speak. If there is no time to it, what do you see?

"I see me without any time attached. It doesn't matter what day, hour or year it is. It is just me."

If that is the case, why do you need a clock?

"So I can keep a schedule."

Now, the question comes to mind, whose schedule is it?

"I could be clever and say it is a relative schedule."

That's clever, but relative to what?

"Problems."

That's correct. Without the influence of problems, there would be no time. So, it seems that what is reflected in the mirror are relative attachments to problems. Now, the reader might say about this time that it seems Seth has gone fairly far afield. But I just took this problem to its linear resolution.

Now, let us take a term that I will call relative co-existence. Without attachment to this relative linearity that you call time, you would be able to step aside and see the plane of other probable realities, or I could say problematical realities in time and discern the relative difference. This is to say that at some time/space intersection or point of light, your viewing would become greater in dimensionality. When you round the corners, you change your consciousness and accelerate the speed of your geometrical mind. A relative idea, let us say a hieroglyph brought forth by ancient Egyptians, can convey an idea on one level and three or more ideas on each harmonic level at a higher vibration. You might say that you have divided the energy of the hieroglyph by harmonic interval and instead of seeing one, you might see seven spread out over time/ space junctures and the one you select is the one that is your reality.

"Excuse me, Seth. As you are speaking, I am seeing some gold and mauve pyramids form on the white paper and it is throwing me off a bit."

Yes, as I am speaking, I am seeking to bring forth by picture the explanation of what I am speaking of. The reader, by something I will call di-tonalism, may pick up a picture or glyph, also. As your radio waves are intercepted by radio sets to display a coherent sound, so are these images conveyed by the same medium to your relative mind.

Now, as you have seen one of these images, let us take the pyramid. Where was it?

"On the paper I am typing on."

What time zone is it in by your clock?

"Now."

I helped you with that answer because this could be conjectured as unexplainable. The image, then, is not in or of time. It just co-exists with your mental frame of mind or mental geometry. The image could be there today, tomorrow or next week. You might say the image is always there if you choose to geometrically intersect with it. When you do not corner yourself, so to speak, you are not trapped in time. You are probably going to ask, "How do you avoid cornering yourself?" And I will say, "Look at the opposite pole to round the square." Do you understand all this?

"Yes, because I saw it as you were speaking of it. The pyramids were here now."

With this embroiderment, we have a jumping off point to something else I have in mind. You have noticed upon some occasions when John has gone to channeling sessions, he hasn't felt well physically. It may have been due to a lack of energy or just that he didn't feel well. Now, beings accept this as being reality. Either you feel well or you do not. So, if you say, "I feel sick", everyone views you as a sick being. If you introduce a miracle, then you may suddenly switch polarity and be a non-sick or well being. Many would say that is a big if. In John's case, upon all occasions, no matter how apparently sick he was, when the channeling session began, he felt fine, no matter what he may have felt prior to this. Several beings who come to your channeling sessions have remarked that spirit can do anything. I wish to explain now that spirit merely brought in a higher vibration and John accepted it, as well as several beings in channeling sessions. You have seen some relative miracles over your time with the influence of energy. What I am trying to get across here is that it is a raise of vibration above the level of the feeling and the negative feeling usually does not come back.

With this in mind, we performed another experiment today. John is in relatively good physical shape with reference to you. Is that not so?

"Yes."

In other words, you regularly exercise and he does not.

"That's true."

Today, I see John took off and walked some ten miles onto a relatively high mountain and came back a few hours later without apparently being worse for wear. You looked a little discouraged when you saw that.

"I work out in a gym, do aerobics and run every day. John does not exercise, yet he is in much better physical shape than I am. That's why I look discouraged."

83

You have this geometrical gadget in the next room that is connected to some frequencies. When it was turned on, what happened, as we write this?

"I feel like I'm floating in a wonderful meditative state."

Let us say that it takes a certain amount of energy to move a mass up a mountain. If it was an automobile, it would be gasoline. If it is a human being, then it might take, supposedly, calories. Does this make sense to you?

"Yes, it does."

Why wouldn't beings run out of fuel relative to an automobile running out of gasoline while expending energy?

"Well, I guess they do."

Apparently, John does not.

"He's not using his energy. He's allowing energy to flow through him instead. That's amazing and seems a lot easier and more effective than what I'm doing."

All right. As we mentioned, we have turned on this geometrical gadget and you feel like you're floating. Where is your energy coming from?

"From that machine."

In John's case, by using a certain amount of energy, he was instantly restored when this machine was turned on. What I am saying here is the machine had the effect of bringing the now moment into both you and John, restoring energy from the infinite source. Someone might argue that it is electricity and I will argue that it is a "light conductor." What has been accomplished with this geometry is the overcoming of the relative limitations of time and space.

If you decide to put your mind in the now moment and throw the idea of past and future aside, there is nearly unlimited energy available to you. What is not admitted currently is the inspiration for the beating of your heart, for instance, and many other body rhythms.

You have just mentioned that the moon appears relatively large tonight and there have been some discussions about your relative cycle going out of balance some two days prior to the full moon. Now, how can you explain this in time?

"I don't know the explanation. I just know it happens regularly."

Might you explain to me that sometimes you appear to be in a cyclical mode?

"I don't know how to answer this question."

Yes, I have tricked you because it would be preponderant of you to come up with an answer using your concept of time. This is a good example of what is that does not have anything to do with time. This cycle might intersect with you at 7:00 AM, 3:00 PM or 2:00 AM. It is not governed by time. Do you see the subtle difference here?

"I still don't know how to answer your question."

The answer comes in angles and cycles of what is, but is difficult for you to describe because of reference to a false concept of time.

First of all, we have to remove the idea of time and space or falsity relative to the higher mind. The higher mind takes these cycles into its stride, but the lower mind does not. At such a juncture, to keep your energy in a positive polarity, you need change your mind by raising vibration or you would suffer a discordant influence upon your personality.

"So, you raise your vibration before you go off the deep end?"

It would be encumbent upon you for your well being to get hold of, let us say, an uncut emerald and wear it two days prior to the full moon. If you are aware of this, but still slip into a negative mode, you could still decide to change your mind and climb out of your negative polarity. The easiest way, of course, is to take measures before this intersection with the moon.

In a probable future book, I will endeavor to explain several techniques for accomplishing this end, but there is not sufficient space here presently.

Now, let us get back to the round circle in the square world. When you seek to force planetary influences into a concept of time that is created by you, you are bound for trouble. You would notice the world happens to be round, not square, and so are most planetary bodies, as well as stars. The concept of taking a round aspect and forcing it into squareness leads one into fear and exhaustion. Someone is working on a project and will not give himself to attempting something else when he is frustrated or tired of it. As he goes on forcing the issue, getting further out of balance, another creation enters and that creation is fear. While this someone is seeking to force his concept of time into a round influence of energy, a round object would start to wobble by the discordant influence of the one who is using excessive force. Does this make sense to you?

"Yes, it does, having just gone through it. The moon is full tonight."

The influence of the planetary body then puts a spherical expression on this plane of reality. As we mentioned, time zones are drawn with relatively straight lines. If you held a giant magnifying lens that covered several miles, how do you think it would influence those beings under this lens? Those who felt the different vibration of light would react differently than those not under its direct influence. If you were

86

to take a colony of ants and blot out the sun, those ants who were on the surface of the ground would temporarily lose their bearings. Now, ants are in the now moment, but beings are not. Beings, especially those living in cities, tend to lose track of these variegated influences and put themselves in a microcosm, supposedly devoid of all other influences. If you close yourself up in a room with no windows, the magnetic lens of the spheres still controls its influence over you. Have you ever thought about this?

"No, I haven't."

Your mind would be only on what you were concentrating on, but what you were concentrating on was influenced by these spheres. Specifically, your powers of concentration would be enclosed by the influence of the magnetic lens.

(After taking a trip, we are resuming this book.)

So, what have you learned relative to time in the other land of your travels?

"Mostly I learned about frequencies and how using them can help you grow and overcome problems."

(Seth leaves the room to change a frequency tape that we are recording.)

I see you have a frequency for guilt.

"Yes, we do."

I thought guilt was an emotion.

"I believe it's a frequency."

Let us say it is both. Do you feel guilty today?

"Not at all."

You may notice that the frequency causes difficulty with you if you are feeling guilt. That is, guilt would

be in the way of the intelligence of the heart. Do you
follow me?

"Yes."

All right then. Tell me where guilt is located.

*"I think it is located in the brain and intelligence is located
in the heart."*

Not bad, but that implies it could be reached in
time by ordinary means and that is a problem. The
location is in the way of the antennae of the head, as
you call it. The "way" is blocked by the gate of guilt.
The recorded frequency your friend gave you pene-
trates the block or gate and opens the door for its
release. But we have a problem here. Do you know
what it is?

*"You have to be willing to open the gate and then find
out how to do it."*

Willingness of course is essential, but relating time
to emotion and frequency seems to be against your
existing laws, isn't that so?

"Yes."

Someone gave you a formula concerning light. Do
you remember what it is?

"Light minus time equals frequency."

You could make a case for continuous frequency if
you were pedantic. So far, this is a relatively meaningless equation, for it will not get you anywhere if
you are stuck in the physical world of time, space or
volume.

Now, this ancient civilization of Indians seemed,
although they were primitive, to know of the existence of a higher reality not currently understood by
modern science. From your experience in some of
their cavaties, you were able to bring forth a higher
reality with just your presence and no additional stim-

ulation from crystals, electronics or other aid. You saw that your lower density emanation, by transferring itself to light, brought you to a greater reality that had absolutely nothing to do with time.

Time stayed still and you changed your reality. What does this tell you?

"Time has nothing to do with reality."

Not only is this correct but it is the block to reality. Since you have seen the incorporation of this frequency which actually breaks up guilt in beings, maybe you could see that each one of these gates of emotion carries you sideways to a parallel volume of time/space.

Since it is difficult to convey feeling to those not feeling the release of entrenched guilt, it would be preponderant to explain further until this idea is absorbed by the consciousness of the reader.

A great percentage of incarnated beings are living with guilt that is hidden and buried away to such an extent that it is currently unrecognizable to them. It masquerades in various elements of fear which only are revealed upon constant attention to the root cause of the driving mechanistic emotion.

You have seen the result of activity by some of your friends in what are affectionately known as "guilt classes." What happened when this was explained and opened to discussion?

"We started remembering things from our childhoods that we felt guilty about."

Which space/time are you referring to, then or now?

"Memories of incidents from our childhoods, when triggered by similar incidents happening now, still cause us to feel fear or guilt."

Give me a time on a specific instance of guilt.

89

"What do you mean?"

It is not understandable, is it?

"I could give you dates for the original feelings of guilt."

Which universe are those in?

"I don't know."

Which time are those in?

"They are in the time that I choose. If I choose to relive those feelings, I am in the original time that I felt them."

There is a problem here, for the concept of time is not valid for such an exercise. Another way to speak of this is, "Where do I put myself?" The only and obvious answer is, "Into another vibration." You could call it a parallel, probable universe. You can already see that by forcing squareness into roundness, one has made a very complex world out of simplicity. If you change your mind and seek to live in emotion from another time, you have also altered your appearance to the degree that you have successfully attached to it. If this was allowed to be carried further, the sense of complexity would be overpowering.

A better way to deal with this increasingly complex emotional time/space plane is to throw out your existing concept of time and use a system of relative vibration. Do you understand me?

"I'm trying."

You can get some idea of where my conciousness is coming from relative to your own from these ideas.

Let us take a system of relative value. A scientist renowned in a particular field, let us say physics, would be currently spending his life postulating and proving theories, never suspecting the artificial boundaries of time that keep him coming back lifetime after lifetime. Beings in general in your current society would give plaudits of praise to such a meaningful lifetime spent in clarifying and educating his fellow society members. In our relative value sense, beauty is in the eye of those assessing judgment. As you can see, it is relative judgment. When the physicist dies, everyone would hold him in high esteem and give little thought to the state of his consciousness.

Someone else who is open to the concept of a greater reality might think twice about such a lifetime and might suppose that energy applied to understanding greater realities might be in their interest.

Time appears relative to your belief system. Do you agree with such a thing?

"I'm a little confused right now."

Is time going faster or slower for your neighbor next door?

"It depends on him."

Good answer and that is exactly what I am speaking of. Now, those beings who, with you, focused on dismembering guilt, caused a relative change in their vibration and their awareness of time. Do you understand how this works?

"Sort of."

By removing a relatively dense part of their focus or emotional attachment from their existing sphere of influence, they relatively lightened their density and increased their rate of vibration.

Look at your body consciousness as being composed of a series of fluids, each with a specific gravity, or another way of putting it, spiral density. Now, what does this mean? It simply means that each body consciousness incarnated here consists of a series of weighted densities creating in sum total your vibration in a given now moment. When each spiral density such as guilt is dismembered or lightened, you then vibrate faster and concordantly would suddenly get that percentage smarter. Do you understand what I mean?

"Yes."

When someone says, "He is a 'chip off the old block', in the context of what we are discussing, they are speaking the truth in all probability. Parents seek to teach the offspring their relative spiral density, thinking it best to pass on the experience they have gleaned. This would purport to be the only way that a sibling could learn. This way of thinking only serves to keep constructed an artificial, relative universe until it is overcome by sheer force of light.

A more efficient source of education is to teach the offspring a system of using greater intelligence inspired from within to bring forth solutions to existing problems devoid of emotion. Such a system would incorporate intelligence not needing the influence of emotion and time.

PURPOSE OF TIME

You can see from the last chapter what this universe is about. There are separated or segmented units that you call time categorized in groups of emotion. Each of these categorized groups of emotion has certain time/space characteristics that can be attributed to it. Using the formula put forth in the previous chapter, you can see the relative density of an emotion and begin to see its percentage purpose in your particular block of time.

Let us take Joe Smith, who with the aid of his greater self, would decide to work on anger. Joe, by some coincidence in his lifetime, has managed to surround himself with a number of highly excitable or angry beings. His wife is known for her lack of tolerance applied along a wide field of interests. In short, it is difficult to get along with her for most other beings. Joe's children, seeing what works for their father and mother, seek in their young lives to apply the same principles of short temperedness. You would say that the stage is set and the play needs to be "played out." Have you ever seen this system of reality?

"Yes, all the time."

So, Joe's family plot consists of anger. How long do you think Joe and his wife will live in years?

"Not very long."

Aha, I expected your answer. And I will tell you it would be relative to the success that Joe and his wife overcome their need to express anger. I could say Joe and his wife will be given all of the time that they need. If Joe's anger draws from his lower emotion, consistently creating heat for his body structure, he will burn up in a relatively short number of years. On Joe's tombstone would be placed, "He was a good man." And no one will think much more about it. Joe's consciousness will undergo intensive training out of time/space and come back for another lesson in anger. To the degree that Joe's wife adjusts her life will be the relative amount of years that she will also spend in the body. You can carry this further and see the wide range of intersections that their influence with anger could beget, but this would be overstating the point.

Let us take another scene at the entrance to a tunnel out of time/space. To be cute about this, let us say a white bearded individual is conducting a final interview by a soul deciding to enter the tunnel or black and white hole of time/space. A set of instructions is being communicated to the soul who will embody at the other end of the tunnel. Previews and reviews are revealed and a probable list of challenges is agreed upon by the soon to be departing soul. Obviously, the picture I am painting seems to be of some physical nature somewhere, however, that is not quite truth, but will suffice for now. Can you imagine such a list that would be given to the probable new incarnate?

"Yes. You said previews and reviews are given beforehand. They already know what is going to happen before they incarnate?"

Yes, they're round and infinite prior to being square and finite. When viewed from expanded reality, you already pre-exist, you see. But when you separate from expansion, you contract into squareness or linearity. Again, the picture is drawn apart line by line, which takes time. Time truly is what you make it. It can be distended and difficult and parallel after parallel as Joe and his family illustrate or it can take on a concept of "Isness" which would be expanded and indefinite. I hope I am not confusing you by these ideas. What do you think?

"It's not confusing. It takes a lot of emotion out of things when you know this. It's pretty funny, actually. I can imagine some of those contracts."

This is similar to a multi-faceted professional athlete's contract, specifying behavior with an indeterminable amount of lifetimes. In other words, you "play ball" until you can laugh about it, laughter being the positive pole of emotion.

There are many families such as Joe's throughout your world. Within every family group, there is another combination of elements or energy that need be worked out. With just the emotions that are known to you, if you merely multiply them times the number of individuals who cross your path on a given day, you will see an enormous number of possibilities. If there is resistance to any of these intersections with other individuals, there will be a corresponding extension of time. Each intersection then allows you a choice on your probable future life. I have endeavored to explain upon many occasions the concept of probable futures because this turns out to be one of the most confusing aspects to beings.

With probable futures, you get into cause and effect and certain laws relating to equilibrium. There is a regular group of individuals that come to your house for channeling sessions with various entities such as I. Over some period of time, you have gotten to know their various aspects of personality. This has become a growth unit or growth family much as like your neighbors next door. Let us call it an extended family

95

unit. Each individual who would compose this unit on a given day or night has certain probable future expectations and they bring them along accordingly. They are endeavoring to create these expectations, both consciously and subconsciously, enabling a process to take place that a friend of yours calls plebiation.

"Did I spell this right?"

Who's going to know if it's right or wrong? One thing about previously undefined terms, no one can argue with them. No heat is generated. No one spends time criticizing. Kidding, of course.

Do you remember what your friend said about plebiation?

"No."

Plebiates can be defined as invisible units emanating from a stone such as limestone, interacting with your bone structure, increasing your vibration. So, I can walk over here and grab this piece of limestone that you use on one of your energetic devices and start plebiating you.

(Seth holds up a piece of limestone, looks at me and says, "Plebiate, plebiate".)

How do you feel now that you have been plebiated?

"Well, I'm laughing, aren't I?"

Then you don't have a "bone" of contention, heh, heh? Well, enough of this. What I really meant to explain was by this process, a being could cause projection from his expectations to jointly affect your future probable time. Let us say that I might make what appears to be an outrageous statement that would be clearly not supportable by scientific fact or any other fact. Within some of your friends' minds could be produced a strange characteristic called doubt. So in effect, silently you would be plebiated by doubt.

"Oh!!"

Why are you ohing?

"Because we have both been uneasy the last couple of days, with a feeling of almost having to explain what we're doing and proving why to a couple of people. This has caused us some unhappiness because we haven't been able to figure out why we are upset. This is like the old knife in the back. You can't see what's causing the trouble, but it's there."

There are many occasions that beings encounter which would not be consciously explainable but still cause the manifestation of physical effects such as sickness and depression.

"What can we do about this?"

Let us take a situation where you wish to take one of your energetic devices to a particular gathering of some religious tribe in a foreign country. Their reaction to you would depend on their particular belief system. There have been rumors upon occasion that you might become the meal of the wrong tribe in the right place. No one would ever say that it does not take courage to allow the physical and mental manifestation of what you are doing to a member of the public.

Remember, for thousands of your years there have been enumerable secret societies which would judge you or deem you ready for execution if you were to go against established society. You already understand that necessarily I need be careful what I write or I will cause you less than divine retribution. When you are plebiated with doubt, cloaked in a thin veil of other raw emotions, the blast hitting you invisibly could have a devastating effect, extending yours and the doubter's time on your plane.

"Why is it so cold all of a sudden?"

97

You are being plebiated, of course. You know in order to write this, you have to live this. Otherwise, I wouldn't be Seth. This way, you do not have doubt and we don't have to go through all of these problems of me proving who I am.

Can you imagine an occasion whereby my voice came in but I wouldn't say who I was? What would you do?

"I would probably know anyway, by the feel of the energy."

What if I masqueraded as another entity?

"I would still know by the feel of the energy, the color I see surrounding John and the rhythm of the speech. I feel it, see it and hear it."

Yes, you feel my vibration. I'm certainly grateful for this because we save much time each day by the fact we do not have to go through guess and tell games for proveability. Imagine this scene. "Hello, I'm, Seth." And you would say, "No, you're not." Then I would say, "Yes, I am." And you would say, "No, you're not!" What would we do then?

"Not much of anything."

Each aspect or volume of time is created by resistance of some sort that may or may not be directed by your greater presence. Remember, there are no exact lines between greater and lesser presence. If the doubter decided that the doubt would take them to another place, that is their free will and choice, isn't it? But you have free will and choice, also, don't you?

"Yes."

You do not have to take in that negativity. There are those who would run into or intersect with you for a period of time that you would jointly and severally agree to experience. When you encounter resistance within yourself, you need to create a mirror that will reflect back to you your behavior. Doubters in some way reflect your fears which you cannot see yourself. To the degree that the doubters fear would be to the degree that your own acceptance is shown.

Now, you could ask how much time this will take. What would your answer be?

"That depends on how much time I want to spend on it once I recognize it and that would be very little time."

Do you need to stop for a cigarette now?

"Yes, thank you. It's still freezing cold in here."

(Seth goes over to the piano and plays something new and different.)

"I didn't know you could play the piano. What did you play?"

Even though it is warm outside, I played cold. That plus the limestone plebiation has lowered the temperature in the room.

"Enough, enough! I believe you're Seth."

Think how the mummies feel.

"I get the point you're making. You can go to any lengths to prove something, but it's time consuming and the effort hardly seems worth it."

To you perhaps, but not others. There is a story in your Bible concerning Moses and the exodus from Egypt, a thinly disguised tale of securing conviction from a doubter. Many religions experience this phenomena. Some beings have such a fixed veil around them that their whole life could be caving in around them and they would steadfastly maintain their point of view.

When you encounter difficulties with opposition to your heart's convictions, notice I did not say ego's convictions, face in the direction of your heart and maintain a steady, northerly direction no matter which way the winds blow. The seed of truth is in the heart of conviction. The seed of truth can shatter the mightiest of fortresses.

Time, then, is extended in all directions simultaneously, filling volume to the point of balance from the causal plane prior to the swing backward after the demunition of the resulting force to the point of light completing the circle. Volumes, then, are the square within the rounded cylinder expanding bidirectionally to form a double pyramid within the circle. Practically, all beings are expanding and contracting time constantly in their attempt to diminish resultant energy falsely attributed to artificial planes sometimes known as astral realms, until their probable emanations are exhausted.

Is it warmer now?

"Yes."

Do you believe it is time for you to experience warmness?

"It must be, because it feels warm in here now."

So, you have intersected with my energy flame, creating another pole of polarity to you called warmth. Do you believe you've created or contracted time?

"I believe I've contracted time. The discordant feeling I had is gone, so my willingness to let go of it brought about its removal with your assistance."

So, you no longer needed to experience coldness in relation to your thought and would therefore allow your volume of time/space to be heated. Do you realize that a room could be 90°F and you could still feel cold?

"Yes, we've experienced this many times."

I know, you're trying to save money for air-conditioning. When you no longer have need for extremes, the resultant swing of your pendulum will be narrower and faster. On each side of the point of light of the swing of the pendulum is expressed the degree of volume or denseness that it is necessary for you to maintain at that given now moment you call time. Remember, in that denseness, you are merely a small fraction of yourself. You might say you are a mere ant of yourself or a mere element of your consciousness of being. One of the confusing aspects in measuring time is apparent size, which eventually you realize is inverted and illusion.

N I N E

EXPLAINING TIMELESSNESS

As many beings as there are currently incarnated are as many reasons and more for the purpose of time. It would serve no purpose to further explain the variety of purposes it is expressing.

The concept of time is the expression of mental geometry manifesting in a volume with certain densities on a wheeled spectrum. The timeless frame is a volumeless or spaceless, multi-dimensional plane of reality that serves on the higher vibrational spiral ending in oneness.

When one speaks in abstract terms of abstract description of something beyond the focus of what you would call ordinary being, one is attempting to describe a foreign object without the conscious knowing of the one endeavoring to understand.

It might be easier to explain the concept ot timelessness by first of all showing my density. Now, I can ask you, what do I, Seth, look like?

"I can't see you."

That is, in your present moment, as far as you know. In several other "past" situations, I have made appearances to your red haired friend and to you. First of all, what did your red haired friend see?

"She saw a short, rotund--I am afraid I will insult you."

Already, we are in trouble, for how can you insult what is not in form?

"But, she saw what you used to look like when you were in form."

So, her projection and my projection made me appear in this form, sitting on a chair at the table in the open room by your channeling session. Now, short, rotund, what else?

"As I recall, she said saw this little short, fat, bald, round-faced person sitting on a chair in the room."

Yes, that is correct. So, I can project the most beneficial appearance that I understand to be the most readily accepted at a given now moment. Now, this reflection which you would regard as my latest or last incarnation is from the one where my veil was the most thin by your standards. Such a projection, while truthful in another time/space, was most useful to bring forth acceptance from your friend. Some say seeing is believing.

Now, on another occasion I used another type of projection that you saw, but have temporarily forgotten. What would that be?

"I see you as tall, thin, handsome, dark haired, purposeful, but humorous and friendly. Our children see you as friendly, also."

So, I have a friendly projection. Upon other occasions, you have seen geometry appear on a paper, as we mentioned before, and light appear on the wall. Does the light appear to come from an unknown source and project through you, casting white and shadow upon your wall? On other occasions, there are slanted rays of light that appear from the ceiling and go to the floor. At other times, a figure slowly appears and progresses along your hallway into the room.

"Yes, I've seen all these things before, during and after the times you come in to dictate these books."

Tell me, where do these projections come from and where am I? Am I up in the sky, am I down in the earth, am I currently residing in some far distant galaxy? Where am I? You have seen upon occasion that I have been "away" for a month or more and would suddenly appear as if no time had elapsed. I did not forget any aspect of you or anything we ever spoke of. Sometimes you may think this is to your detriment, that I would use such knowledge against you.

Excuse me, it is time, so to speak, for you to create your timeless water, using red and green.*

So, maybe you can say you are making timeless water for the beings' use in channeling. But back to what we were talking about. If I become timeless in your eyes or perception, I would become volumeless or formless. But since I am speaking to you, you might say that I am here and I am there. Or, I (positive) Am (negative) combining the aspects of gender, transforming myself or a proportion of myself to your octave.

If you would go outward in a space ship looking for me, you could not go fast enough because you would be limited by your consciousness to some relative form of the speed of light. You could say that by preconceived notions of reality that you limit yourself to certain conditions of reality that you have created.

Now, it might seem from some of the foregoing chapters that I would be taking aim at various scientific aspects of your society, but that is not where I am

*Each Wednesday night, a small group gets together at the McAuliffe house for an energetic channeling session. Depending upon the vibration needed, water is charged in the sun with colored gels, sometimes stones, and a burst of magnetic energy that is used to alter the vibrations of those in channeling who drink it.

placing the energy. Where I am seeking to promote change is the residency of the preconceived notion proclaiming that this density of some 186,000 miles per second is the limit of your reality. By this very notion, I do not exist and therefore am not writing this book. By this very notion, you are writing it. Somehow, someplace, something is wrong with this idea. Now, I do not mean to take issue with everyone reading this book, but am taking issue with the preponderance of thought that has caused separation resulting in time.

I wish to discuss something that I will call the Law of Harmonic Intention. For want of another term, this idea seeks to explain the harmonic multiplication of channels, meditation, dreams, projections and other forms of intuition not explainable by physical law currently known. If John as a channel *(strongly spoken)* has intention to bring forth unmitigated truth from All That Is, then the harmonic reverberation or reflection from All That Is, known as Seth, will reflect accurately and truthfully within the limits of consciousness of the receiver. What I am stating is that by exact application of what you would call higher law, an angle of reverberation would phase in a higher reflection of energy reflecting itself within your sphere. Your universe or sphere of time is merely out of phase with other dimensions of time. All intelligence would seek to have you express as your higher reflection and lower reflection fits into the energy available to you at present.

The winds of change are indeed expressing a change in the current idea of materialism. This is no fiendish plot conceived by the higher order to cause harm to unsuspecting humans. Souls choosing to incarnate at this age have chosen the general experience, as many know, to witness the transition into a more harmonious age.

As the reader reads this book, a certain geometric expression of ideas is realized that takes on the imaginative consistency that you would reflect and know as this book called "Timelessness." This is to say that reading causes your mentality to paint pictures in the form of gender that is positive or negative, registering your impression and causing you to register your statement where you are receiving the vibrations at a given now moment. If two months from now, you read this very same book again, you will find that a different impression is registered upon your being or mentality and it may even seem like it is a different book entirely, written at a different time. Cell memory is short, which is to say ego memory can be relatively short and unless it makes a strong emotional impression that I eluded to in my Ascendent Thought book, it is promptly forgotten except by your greater self. It isn't that the memory is gone. It is buried so deeply and without sufficient charge to render it inaccessible at a given moment. If this were not so, beings would generally grow rapidly enough that they would soon shake free of the volume of their time/space.

What happens to you if for any reason you have to re-read another one of my books?

"I did that very thing a few weeks ago and it was as though I was reading it for the first time, even though I was very involved in the writing of it, having typed and proofread it before it was printed."

It is hoped that the readers will read between the lines, taking their own ideas for the construction in their own mind of what I am suggesting to them.

You have two friends, D. and C., who have a relatively small house and yet, when you go in the various rooms, by a particularly clever use of geometric space, the house appears larger inside to your mind than would a conventional house of the same size. An impression is formed with the geometric caves that are open in a section of the ceiling causing a different frequency to reside in the rooms than would be there without the addition of the hollowed out sections. The room, with the four walls, floor and ceiling is one frequency and a harmonic is created when you add additional rectangular space cut into the ceiling. You are causing a different time and space to flow when you create such an opening. When you walk into someone else's house, you get certain impressions with color, design, etc., but possibly would be unaware of the geometric configuration that resonates with your mind. What is a "modern" house to you?

"A house with a lot of open space, many windows, clean, straight lines, light colors--"

(Seth interupts me.)

I didn't ask for a book. What if the house were built in 1933?

"That would probably be pretty depressing to me. I like new houses."

Would you say, then, that the house is time dated?
"Yes."

What about calling it vibration dated? You can see already that something would be put into a context of time automatically. Your mind might have trouble if a 1933 house was built with modern material reflecting the old design. It would probably throw your psyche off somewhat, resulting in a "category-less" confusion. Have you ever had category confusion?

"What is that?"

I'm glad you asked because that is what happens when you try to put what you regard as the wrong time in the right place. Or is it the right time in the wrong place?

With this idea, you can begin to see, if you do not pass over these sentences too quickly, that there is some time/space confusion in the mind when it attempts to compartmentalize into a limited system that continually creates confusion with its falsity.

"Some people like older houses. Do they like a different vibration?"

Yes, cellular memory has resulted in the attraction of a certain geometry that fits into their category. Now you know what beings mean when they say, "I categorically deny this." Aren't you glad that we cleared up this confusion for you? That is to say I cannot place it into one of my preconceived categories, therefore I must deny it.

How can you create a category in the past that seeks to compartmentalize in the future that does not exist in the now moment? If I was a being and tried this sort of thing, I probably would create the problems of fear, insecurity, hate, jealously, etc. Wouldn't you agree?

"Yes."

So, these ideas of fear would seek to fill the gap between past and future called time. Do you fully understand what I am suggesting?

"I almost have it."

All right, here is a situation where you would create time. Let us say that a salesman comes to your door and puts enough pressure on you to buy some object that the only way you can effectively deal with him is to postpone a decision on buying the object until, let us say, one week from then. After the salesman leaves, you feel guilty for not dealing with him directly at the time and saying no. You didn't want to hurt his feelings so you therefore postponed your decision into your subconscious until a later date. At that time of postponement, you create time to fill the span built between the time of making the decision of postponement until a probable, future time. Between the time that the salesman comes back to your door and the original meeting, guilt or time/guilt was created to fill the gap in your mind. With this creation, you have extended your time and have extended the time of your whole universe to a small degree.

Using this one example, think how many creations go on consistently in the minds of beings failing to directly deal with stimuli at a given now moment.

Someone early in life discovers that they enjoy painting or creating some object. They are so enamored with their creations that they go on creating until their body is worn out and they pass on seeking to re-experience this or similar creations in other lifetimes until such time as they desire other experience or atonement. Do you understand this?

"This appears a little different from your other ideas of compartmentalization. I'm confused."

Now that I finally have you stopped again so we can resume, you can see then, as with the houses, you would have what I might call a compartmentalized mind. If each segment or compartment of your mind is composed of storage units called frequencies, then you can see that any falsity would be composed of a lower density frequency giving you access to breaking it up if you wish. Why did you get so confused?

"I don't know what happened. I couldn't figure out what you were asking me and I was even having trouble trying to type what you were saying. I couldn't understand you."

Do you suppose I "inadvertantly" triggered some geometric reasoning within you that opened some of these chambers or compartments?

"You must have because I couldn't figure out what was going on."

You have noticed that occasionally I use certain energy that causes you and other beings to speak in a certain way or to act or feel things in a certain way. Cause and effect or stimulus response might serve to explain this energy. What is energy composed of? It is composed of relative degrees of feeling, taste, sense, smell, light, sound. These are vibrations that cross your physical sense line or vibrational density of your existence. Other aspects of this energy in faster harmonics are invisible to your physical senses and would be deemed to belong to the timeless element. Now, there is some room for discussion here, for some frequencies may appear to be invisible but are still measureable by instruments. These may also intersect your plane, causing change of sense. Some might call this non-sense. I only thought I would be sensible.

How can you measure the time of your reflection? Do you know?

"No."

How much time on your clock will it take a reaction from one of your mirrored images to appear in your life? I know you have no way of answering this question. An answer to such a question is, to the relative number of your vibration would degree the relative swiftness at its return to you in the form of a mirrored image. If you do not project any emotion into your creations, the low level of their trajectory may throw them into infinity not circling them back as your mirror. Do you follow me?

"Yes. If you don't put out any emotion, you won't attract any negativity back."

There are those who do not appear to have what you would call a "conscience" who seem to act with impunity. In other words, if you do not put your etheric rubber band onto one of your creations, it may not spring back to you. In essence, then, you would be creating in a timeless vein. Beings you would know as masters may appear to be creating from emotion, but in essence have placed no attachment to their creations and therefore would be creating by the higher law of the timeless realm. Is that clear to you?

On another matter, it would be interesting for those wishing to experiment with mental geometry to try the following experiment. Cut out a white circle, a green triangle and a red square. They could be up to two feet in diameter with the lines an inch or two wide maximum. Select your favorite room in your house and start with the red square up on the wall for one or two days at eye level in the center of it. Once you have pinned it on your wall, make an effort to forget that it is there for two days. On the side, when you are not in the room, check your mood when you were in the room and make a note or two.

Next, place the green triangle upon the wall and leave it for three days, observing in the exact manner as you did with the red square. Keep track of your observations. Next, place the white circle upon the wall, this time for five days, making the same observations while you are out of the room. I assume that if you have a white wall, you would put some kind of background contrasting the white circle from the white wall. Or, if you have a green wall, then you would put a different colored background behind the triangle, etc.

Now, I am not going to spoil your fun by suggesting exactly what it is that you will find, but the ancients have tested such a procedure and inform me that it is most interesting, along the lines of viewing your moods in a timeless vein.

Energy flows in through your system that you call a zodiac in the effect of a spiral that looks like a strung out comma. Energy seeks to leave the self-same system by another inverted comma that is the reverse of the first. You might call this yin-yang. Some of the temples in your ancient civilizations, such as Egypt, were set up in such a fashion. But closer to home, so are you. What I mean to imply, energy is consistently flowing in and flowing out in lower, slower cycles and higher, faster cycles relative to you. The ancients sought to intersect or channel these cycles into their consciousness by intercession, using their objects or monuments to re-emerge their consciousness with the higher unknown planes of consciousness.

Sitting outside at night viewing an energetic star such as Sirius or Canopus will enable your consciousness to take in simultaneously several distinct spirals of energy if you open your mind to receiving them. Many beings would take a look at a star and say, "Oh, there it is. I identify you." The astronomers say, "If it is in this location and in this pattern and in this time, it must be Sirius," then dismiss it after a few minutes. They may become bored at this time and walk away saying, "That was pretty. Now I will go back to doing my taxes or reading my mystery novel." There is nothing wrong with either of these activities, however, understanding the former or star gazing takes a little more effort. First of all, the ancients had a different conception of what education was about. If you were a philosopher, sage or what you might call an educated being, you not only knew astronomy but you also knew astrology, chemistry, medicine and politics. You, as such an educated person, did not seek to isolate your knowledge into separate compartments of specialization.

Did you know that beings are so specialized today that sometimes they nearly "reinvent the wheel" only to find out that their neighbors down the block have the exact knowledge that they are seeking. The ancients would seek to have all of the knowledge under one roof, which happened to have hair on it, usually, except in my case. Heh, heh. The ancients, staring at a star such as Sirius did not seek to limit their knowledge to one area or compartment such as astronomy and attempted to incorporate what they had observed about Sirius across a wide field of interests including the higher plane of intuition. When something of an inner disciplinal nature was observed and it did not seem to coalesce with what they knew, it was not deemed inappropriate to meditate on the mystery. A discussion with others of similar vibration often proved quite fruitful.

I see that something different is happening today, that there is not the sharing among different disciplines that there was among the ancients. Today it is seen that there is competition among disciplines to arrive at the "correct" solution of a problem that incorporates their discipline only. It would not be deemed politically expedient to have an astronomer solve a medical problem. He might be regarded as suspicious for intervening in a discipline not his own. And much energy would be directed toward him to stick within his own realm of knowledge. Many brilliant individuals, as you would regard them, have been stifled in their endeavors into areas other than their field of study.

But back to Sirius. What did you see when you observed this star?

"I saw it turn green, red and blue."

Whose eyes were you seeing with?

114

"Mine."

One of these colors is observed in this plane and others in another plane of reality. As you extended your eyes further, not knowing that you cannot see such a thing because it doesn't exist, you saw something else take shape. What was that?

I saw the stars form the shape of a dog."

Why are you hestitating?

"To tell you the truth, I was worried about something. I did see the shape of a dog, but I don't know if it was correct, in accordance with what is shown on the star maps."

In other words, you feel you might be criticized.

"Correct."

I now brand you a nut. Now, you see what is a problem in the age you live in. It would be the squelching of knowledge unless it is politically acceptable. In ancient Egypt, for instance, as well as the ancient Mayans or Incas, observations of this nature were valued by the ruling elite and would be investigated strongly for possible insight into the infinite. Practical use was made of these observations and temples were built accordingly to overcome disease, to gain insight into sometimes remarkable abilities that would deem such individuals God-like today. Even in those societies, certain individuals, by their mental prowess, were treated as Gods. A marked propensity toward this insight would be rewarded concordantly.

Now, watch the cycles of the star, Sirius, as it intersects at various angles of your horizon and observe its behavior both when it is low on the horizon and higher in elevation. The various cycles that resonate with you at the various times of year and/or night are consistent with the pattern that promoted the use of ancient calendars. The use of a calendar which has as its implication, time, was developed by a lower civilization to enable the then residents of an area to keep track of various seasons to gather water, grow food and perform certain rituals which were deemed to bring in higher energy. When all was by degree or angle, it enabled the ancient ones, by use of their astronomical observations, to overcome fear of the sometimes hostile elements and to be able to predict years in advance the probable onset of a hostile environment such as an ice age or exceptionally wet year, to enable them to be better able to survive. Calendars by geometric observation would have taken untold eons of experience without the higher intuition used to bring forth the new knowledge.

Think today of a world that would suddenly encompass another way of thinking and being such as that of the ancient Egyptians. All known religions and political systems would be foreign to the ideas of the ancients. There would be little use for technology in their system of reality. Theirs was a system of mind seeking to incorporate harmonics of all levels and by any means available to replicate them in their visible lifetime. What do you think of an Egyptian concept of time and why would I bring this up?

"I don't know the Egyptian concept of time."

Do you think they would have need for a watch?

"Only if they all had them. It is strange that you are mentioning this because our daughter came walking in wearing a new pair of shoes that had non-working watches on them. This is a strange coincidence."

It's a strange time. Categorizing units such as emotion into time has only served to separate and confuse.

"You forgot to tell us the Egyptian concept of time."

116

There wasn't one. Time only becomes necessary to fill the void between past and anticipated events. Otherwise, why would it be needed? If one decided to let go and wait for the solution to a difficulty or problem, the solution rendered in harmony would float in with much more force than one created by the force of the moment in time. When one forces a solution because one is under artificial space/time pressure, one usually renders a partial solution and many times would have well waited to speed up the result.

Let us get into geometry for a moment. If you look at a triangle such as the 1-2-3 triangle of the Egyptians, using a 36° angle and a side of 72 parts, the proportions inherent in this geometrical object produce or cause to tie in lines of force that interconnect with higher planes of reality. Use of this object can cause a flow of energy that tends to break up the visible spectrum of light promoting at least a higher vibration in meditation and accelerating the level of dreams. I do not mean to suggest a proliferation of gadgets, but a discussion of an idea. Trying such an object as you put together in a rather rough fashion caused a glow of sorts and a distension of angles of light that would be difficult to know unless you had seen them. This being a basic building block of your universe, causes an oscillation bringing forth minor phenomena but useful to your expansion of energy. Why would I bring such a thing up in reference to timelessness?

"It would assist me in changing my mind."

Whatever do you mean?

"My system of values would change."

Whose system is it?

"The one I have been taught."

Now, this may seem odd, but where you would have a former attraction perhaps to a new car, you might now be attracted to some old ruins. You might say such an object might ruin your life. Many beings reading this might say, "I would have no intention of doing such a thing. What kind of an idiot would try such a thing anyway? Why would they do such a thing? Probably the same nut that would see space ships."

"Seth, what are you trying to do, ruin us?"

You mean you don't want to act like an Egyptian?

"No, I mean I don't want you to tell anybody we act like Egyptians."

Now we are getting into an area devoid of time that is called happiness.

Let us take a mythical family known as the Hoteps. This is differentiated from Smith and Jones, not that anything is wrong with Smith or Jones. The Hoteps enjoyed this civilization to the degree that they were capable, both with good jobs, two new cars, one a foreign beauty and at least two children. Their house was resplendent, in a newer section (time), in a large city in any state, U.S.A. All seemed well with the Hoteps, who were in their early forties. They thought they were absolutely happy, but after a relatively few years of this, boredom crept in. Something was missing. They bought a dog. More boredom. They bought a boat. More boredom. They joined a theater company. More boredom. They began to fight. No more boredom, but the health of the adults began to deteriorate and even though there was apparently nothing externally wrong, something was not right and visible signs of external aging were preponderant. What to do. It is incumbent upon one to do something, otherwise you would run out of time. One of

118

them said, "Let's take a trip while we're still embodied." The other said, "Where?" After a brief fight, it was decided to go to Egypt to view the scenery. Anything was better than fighting. While there in Egypt, they suddenly found the love of their lives--ruins. Some might say their lives were already in ruins, however, an infusion of energy literally entered their bones. It was decided due to the change of scenery, that possibly they might change their lives. I guess you could say the old looked better than the new. And there was a time/space difficulty. Everything in their lives took on renewed vigor and it wasn't long before jobs were changed, new education came forth and attitudes changed completely. After several trips to the ruins, they decided to write a book which was completely different from anything they ever did in their previous occupations. Some of the energy from the ancient temples revived an area of their minds, both with frequency and with geometry and the aging process which was leading them into rapid deterioration into bad health, was arrested and their energy returned.

From the foregoing, where did this time/space come from? Oh, I forgot to add, the Hoteps are now living in Cairo, Egypt and their children speak Egyptian and have never been so happy. There's only one place it can come from which is the intersection with the higher plane and the lower plane. That is the mind. You change your mind and you change time.

In our story, several voids were created upon the termination of the need for time/space which you call experience. Many beings will go forth and continue beyond the usefulness of a particular activity because they are too fearful to take the chance and change into an area where the universe will pour forth new energy inspiring new direction. Where does energy come from? You attract it by creating a void. When your past is rapidly becoming your future and you are fearful and bored, it would behoove you to seek to fill the void with a new activity which seemingly will generate energy from nowhere. Do you have an explanation of timelessness, then?

"Yes."

T E N

UNDERSTANDING TIMELESSNESS

It serves no useful purpose to bring forth lofty principles from a higher plane not understood by readers, leaving them in the same position in which they began at the start of the book. By the use of stories and other symmetrical means to distract the ego which purports to know all that is about time, I would serve to illustrate from my plane what your plane looks like.

Viewing beings in various modes of expression would have me seeing you in many bodies at once. If I viewed an object from my plane, I could intersect with it geometrically and I could see a series of freeze-frame pictures of a being walking down a street. While viewing you as a being, I would also see the cloud broken up around you in your many moods or hues, changing reflection with each advancing or receding picture as you step. If I wished to intersect with a being such as you or John, I would seek to contact you in a frame of mind that would help you and I at the maximum of our joint expression. By my contact with you, your probable future in time alters to the degree of our joint expression and will accelerate your vibration to the degree that we jointly create a mutual oneness.

Use oneness to perceive nowness or the now moment, devoid of time. There is harmony where there is no time. You might say, "But Seth, what about beautiful music? There is harmony there." And I would have to remind you that the beautiful music already is. You are merely unwinding it, frame by frame, line by line, so that your physical ear can perceive. What you are doing, in effect, is slowing down higher harmony that already is and expressing it in your plane.

The plot created in the last story already pre-exists in many time/space dimensions and only need be played out in your conscious realm to enjoy the experience. As has been stated by others, a miracle is a change in a time/space intersection. Another way of saying this is it is the use of a higher law that is unknown to you in a lower plane. Who are you? You are the sum total of your existing experiences, usually those that you are currently accessing.

At any given time or maybe by this time when you use the now moment, you are a given construction of ideas that are broadcasting in some form at what you might call an angle of light. Let us reflect on an issue that might be categorized as coming from a higher plane. Let us take something you might call divine image. What is a divine image to you?

"A picture of Jesus the Christ, complete with aura and rays of light."

Many beings would have this image, but what I was really driving at is, the reflection to a degree that you will allow it, is really a projection of you. Did Jesus the Christ look a certain way? Do you have a photograph? No, of course not. It would only be a symbolic painting or an image in your mind. The rays of light and the idea of someone on a higher plane, for reasons that would be difficult to explain, are raising your own vibration to the percentage that you are capable of receiving. It has been said, I Think, Therefore I Am. You could go further with this and state, I Am, Therefore

I Project. Projection is across the space separating mankind from the divine. A cross is a symbol for the bridge that seeks to cross, so to speak, this gap or bridge the gap. Words are symbols. Ideas cause symbols to form.

"I just felt a burst of energy go through my head from left to right. It almost made me dizzy and I'll have to ask you to repeat the last sentence. I missed it."

You can see how this gray, shall we call it, ghost of energy was transmitted to assist you in understanding the bridge concept. Someone in a technical occupation might encounter a problem defying description to the extent that it might be easier to explain by something they might call divine coincidence. Certainly that would not be acceptable and would be dismissed accordingly if the thought arose.

If someone happened along at that time and struck up a conversation with the technical one and mentioned in the conversation something of God and church, then the technical one would be open to accept the idea of churchism and would open the compartment in the mind associated with churches and there would be no problem speaking of the divine. Does this make sense to you?

"Yes."

When the ancients spoke of balance, they spoke of it in a different way than is thought of today. Balance incorporates a kind of flotation whereby a hollow glass sphere in water will float. If you filled the glass sphere with mercury, it would not float. The ancients gleaned body, mind and spirit in some proportion that was constantly, chemically, electrically and energetically seeking to attain harmony. They had a kind of knowing sense that enabled them to intuit that they might need to injest copper, for instance, or cinnamon, or

123

eat an orange. They further knew that if they were out of balance too far with one type of work, that their body would suffer unless they switched their focus. It could be some sort of restful activity would be needed, such as meditation or watching the wind blow across the water. I believe there are laws in your society that prevent this sort of behavior. Is that so?

"There are laws in our minds that prevent it."

Oh, you're catching on. Now, I wish to go into a little more detail regarding another type of balance and that is the balance between intellectual intelligence and timeless or intuited intelligence. As each soul incarnating has a certain map or purpose (probable purpose), then each civilization has kind of an overall plan or purpose. One type of civilization, such as yours, would be heavily focused in the intellectual realm, placing high value on intellectual attainment. Let us call this intelligence of the head and it is thus timed. The other type of intelligence, of course, is timeless and is everywhere and in everything and is drawn upon through the heart. So, you have intelligence of the head and of the heart, timed and timeless. The dividing line is in the throat, of course. If you are floating about in your theoretical glass sphere, you will phase into another realm and more of you will be focused in the relaxed or heart state. You could say maybe I'm speaking a little of something like meditation, but not exactly. Your mind has nearly infinite states of consciousness that are overlapping. Like ocean waves, one wave overlaps another and so it is with consciousness. In your society, the head intelligence or intellectual attainment is far, far out of balance with the aims of the heart. What is one of the greatest health worries at present?

"Heart disease."

Do you think this might be a remarkable coincidence once it is pointed out?

(The cat jumps up. Seth puts her down, trying to be kind so the cat doesn't feel rejected.)

"Yes."

As you see, with compartmentalized or timed intelligence, much can slip by just beyond the gates of a particular compartment and what is taking place right around the corner escapes your attention. Lifetime after lifetime could be spent in one or more of these compartments. There have been many cases in your society whereby beings are so focused on individual, intellectual attainments that nearly all other aspects of what you might call body consciousness are allowed to disintegrate. You know of some of these individuals. Some of them work in hazardous occupations, let us say handling dangerous chemicals. And you might say to some of them, why do you do such a thing? What would their answer be?

"The job pays well and offers many benefits."

Then you might tell them, "But it's killing you." Then what would they say?

"They would ignore my question. They don't realize what they are doing."

Someone such as I, in a channeling session, might ask someone in such an occupation if he thought it was dangerous. The first time I asked the question, he might not even think about it and give me a half-compartmentalized answer and let it go. If I let time go by, let us say two years from that now moment, then asked the same question again, an odd thing may happen. He suddenly might become fearful and realize the hazard to his body that he rather haphazardly was causing. At that point comes a change and he

125

comes out of his compartment and takes a look around. What do you think happens then?

"Then the person would be upset because he has to make a change now that he knows something is wrong."

At this time, there is a change of time by change of mind and then the heart at the throat opens up. You are looking at me strangely.

"Because I'm on the edge of discovering something, but I don't have it yet."

Have you ever heard of beings relating stories where they felt their heart in their throat?

"Of course, many times."

Someone, then, pours out "his heart" to you. There are songs relating to various castigations of the heart. Let us say the throat, which has the voice box in it, can reflect heart or head intelligence. So you can speak the truth through your voice box or you can stretch the truth through your voice box. Do you see what I mean?

"Yes. Is the throat a reflector?"

Why yes. It is your power center whereby you reflect lower or higher intelligence. There have been many stories written of long necked creatures that purportedly were on the path to illumination—ibises, swans, etc. The sacredness of the ibis as held by the Egyptians seemed to have something to do with them making rather odd sounds at strange times. That is, in times of illumination, the bird would purport to make a rather odd sound, maybe a symbol for a time of divine illumination. The throat has a certain resonation that in a sense, would defy the resonator to squelch the source of the resonating intelligence.

When someone is speaking to you, there are little, nearly inaudible frequencies that vibrate which will reveal the true resonation of the speaker. If the speaker is nervous, guilty, etc., there will be tiny, harmonic break ups in the voice that tell the truth behind the words. Do you understand what I am saying?

"Yes."

Give me an example of such a thing, then.

"The voice sounds strained, not a smooth cadence."

There are instruments you can purchase that will detect these nearly inaudible resonations as a kind of truth meter for those needing such an apparatus.

Speaking of things out of time, the design of your floor tile is taken from a design of the ancient Mayans.

"I knew it was meaningful."

Now, don't get carried away. When one first tentatively becomes aware that the overall goals society purports to lay down to an individual may have compensating balances, then one has opened the door of their compartment. You realize I am not suggesting revolution, but merely to put on another set of eyes. You might call me four eyes, two timed, two non-timed. This starts taking on an aspect that the ancients brought forth as dualism. Now, let us take Dotti 1 and Dotti 2. Dotti 1 is humorous, happy, bright and delightful. Dotti 2 is angry, resentful, morose and sleepy. There rarely is a time where there would be all Dotti 1 in place or all Dotti 2 in place. Right now, on a percentage basis, where do you seem to fit?

"70% of 1, 30% of 2."

So, when I look at you, I see twins and two clocks. Do you understand me?

"Two clocks at the same time?"

Two clocks at different speeds or different angles. So, you are then, categorically speaking, 8:00 Dotti and 5:00 Dotti. As you shift your focus, you pull in attributes of each. Why are you yawning? I am talking about you.

"Sorry, I can't seem to stop yawning."

(Seth walks into another room and comes back with a picture of John and, unknown to me, it has a gold, water-filled glass vase in the background that seems to have reflected the sun. Seth next picks up the same vase with water in it, sets it on the typewriter, then proceeds to shake it in front of my eyes and stops dictation. I go outside at this time and have a cigarette, having glanced at the mirror as I was going outside, thinking how awful I look.)

(When I come back in and sit down at the typewriter, Seth asks me to go over and look at the mirror. Upon looking in the mirror, I realize that I look much better. I then come back to the typewriter. Seth has not said anything about this, except for asking me to look in the mirror.)

What do you think is behind what I just did and you just did?

"A change of vibration?"

I shook up your thoughts and helped you turn them into golden ones. How do you feel now?

"I feel better."

Do you have any idea why this would be?

"Some gold was injected into my sphere of influence."

The Mayans and other ancient peoples realized the true value of gold was its timeless essence of vibration. Many metals are used up and more ore is dug up, more metal is smelted and the process goes on and on. Gold and some other rare metals are different in that they are used over and over by remelting and reforming. The form taken is only a reflection of the time. Gold, in its physical essence, is more strongly reflecting the time and timeless aspect of itself. Naturally, all metals have other harmonics associated with them, but gold is different, being the strongest vibration resonating in your physical sphere. You might say you have taken on essence of gold or golden image. It nearly goes without saying, then, that gold is the timeless aspect of an individual's being.

The energy aspect from the timeless realm seeks to flow in direct reference to the subject of growing into oneness. Now, you and John were both wondering what that means. If you think of a divine aspect, you literally take on a golden tinge in your surrounding field. There are those who would say, "I cannot see such a thing. Seth, this is outrageous." If you will bear with me a bit and use some type of test such as we conducted with the vase of water, you will feel the flow of energy that is "contacted" when you bring forth the divine. It is mentioned in writings here and there that at a certain point in your spiritual progress, objects will start to have a faint glow. You are merely seeing the higher harmonics of energy emanating from an object. You might reference it to the spectrum of light from the sun projected through a quartz crystal upon the wall. Light is divided into individual frequencies and you call it color. Your own reflector or higher mind divides out light, also, and the projection of such is called an aura, a divine emanation or spectrum of light that happens to emit from yourself or another that you view. What this is, in effect, is you setting aside your aspect of "can'tism" and allowing that such a thing may exist and you would give it a try. Naturally, you can do this privately, as you may not wish to risk the criticism of those who "know" better.

Another simple way of coming to an understanding with this type of energy is to look into a mirror in a relaxed position with a light background behind you

129

and see if, surrounding you, may come a slight hint of a light emanation. Don't tear yourself apart if at first you don't succeed.

There have been those beings who come to you in channeling and say, "I just don't see anything. I never have and I probably never will." Do you know of these beings.?

"Yes, I do."

What usually happens after they have insistently denied any ability to see?

"Sometimes, after the subject changes, they relax and while off guard, they "accidently" start describing things they are seeing."

Yes. It might range anywhere from odd colors on the wall to flashes of light. The phenomena of the compartmentalization of denial is an important one to beings. As long as one assures everyone that you are quite sane, thank you, by denying any such ability, then it is all right to go ahead and state what you see. This phenomena is like unto the technical being who we spoke of previously, whom you could not get to admit any phenomena in his work, but then could talk of God and church in a separate conversation. Did something click there?

"Oh, yes. I just came to the understanding of what you have been talking about with the compartmentalization."

This is a very tricky concept and one that I have taken pains to ensure that you grasp. Mentioning further would be the aspect of physical seeing in the physical world as you know it. Some days your vision might be measured as 20-10 at a distance. Other days it may be 20-20. There is not an exact measurable vision, but one that varies from day to day, hour to hour and minute to minute. What do you think your mind does from now moment to now moment?

"It varies."

Yes. If you took, for instance, a college entrance examination, one day you may score a very high number and if you should happen to take it again, you might score a different number, perhaps a low number. The concept of bio-rhythms purport to take into account your physical and mental condition at a given time. Everyone seems to know something of them, but no one has an exact definition. They take into account your cycles with reference to astronomical cycles of the planets, moon, sun and stars. I don't wish to get into an extended discussion of this important aspect of your geometric being, but it influences your time/space concept to an important degree at a given time. I will get into this concept in a probable future book and explain how to use higher law to circumvent their influence on your plane of reality.

An interesting dream sequence happened to you and John yesterday in reference to the time and timeless planes of reality. Do you recall the dream?

"Yes."

Your dream had you in a dark hole in the ground and you were seeking to climb out into an expanded, lighter condition. You felt claustrophobic while trapped in the hole and, of course, made great effort to free yourself.

John's dream had you sleeping in an apartment, both of you wearing white bathrobes. Surrounding the apartment was what you might call a modern shopping center, consisting of many levels of nothing but clothing stores. As John walked around in a conscious state, other beings were coming up escalators in a robot-like state, heading toward various clothing stores to purchase various articles of clothing. John was wandering around among them and one of them even spoke to him, but was in a deep, trance-like state, barely able to even notice John. None realized they were in a robot-like state. Each time John closed a door, more beings came forth to try to find additional racks of clothing to purchase. Finally, there was no place further to go and some robot-like beings were moving a bed in to sleep in the middle of what was now clothing racks.

At this time, John saw a tiny dog on top of a chest of drawers and the dog was waiting for affection in anticipation. As John picked the dog up, it ran away down the hallway and John realized that it was the only "real" appearing thing in the dream.

Now, as we took a brief break, you brought up something quite interesting. What was that?

"I think the dog in the dream was Sirius, the Dog Star. It was sitting on a chest of drawers. The heart is in the chest and it is through the heart that energy flows into the cavities in our bodies, which were symbolized by the drawers of the chest."

Yes, you are quite clever. It's a good thing I am not in competition with you or I would deny everything in my compartment.

"Was the obsessive buying of clothes an attempt to cover up who the people really were, the clothing of denial?"

Now, before anyone takes this to mean that it is wrong to go shopping for clothes, this is far and away again, not the point. It has been stated by some that one man's dream is another man's reality. It is also mentioned from place to place that mankind is walking around asleep and will one day awaken. This is the concept that would be suggested by the dream and why I wished to see it included as an explanation of timelessness.

Mankind in general, as I have already mentioned, is not exactly going along in a sleepy state, but one fixated in compartmentalized states of being that have the doors sealed by lack of awareness of what is taking place immediately beyond their present thoughts. Many are so enraptured by their activities that their only view of anything beyond themselves would be by accident and would be regarded as an intrusion and a disturbance. The mere suggestion of anything beyond their core of reality that they have created would be deemed an insult not provable scientifically and an unwarranted intrusion upon their privacy. Words such as, "I demand you prove the existence of something I do not know or I will not give it any attention at all," clearly show resistance to any non-compartmentalized thought.

It appears that I am using rather strong or harsh words to describe this situation, but I really wish to draw the attention of the reader to something that many little suspect. In the dream, there were those wandering about, seeking to fulfill themselves by purchasing a covering in a robot-like trance. That seemed like a sequence from a dream world. If this picture can be taken in without bias, there is something important going on here that is beyond the normal consciousness of the individual. Immediately beyond the shopper is another, higher plane of reality that is timeless, that is expanded and is witnessing the shopper shopping to fulfill a need that he knows not what it is. Many seek to fulfill themselves by purchasing objects that they have little or no use for. Many others seek to fulfill themselves by boring activities that they have no idea how to replace with viable understanding.

Just beyond, sometimes witnessed in the dream state, is the existence of an expanded state of being

133

that you little suspect, in another field of consciousness. Slowly, I am seeking to have you discover this greater aspect of reality that is left when the supposedly important sense of "doing" life runs out of steam. There the colors on a given day are brighter. There the sense of well-being is known. There the start of a sense of oneness is gleaned. There the projection into millions of happy beings is brought about. Do you understand what I am trying to convey?

"Yes. You are waking us up."

Each scene, each situation has its many facets. Let us call them negative, neutral and positive. You could have the same scene being played in three separate households surrounding you and depending upon the resident amount of emotion would decide the category with which you replace them. Each stage play is a creation of time, but of different lengths. Do you understand what I mean?

"Yes, I do understand."

Let us get into illustrations in the timeless realm of oneness. You went to some stores yesterday, yourself. John said he drew some runes totaling the number 47 before you left. What happened in each store where you went?

"Our bill at the grocery store was $47.00. Our bill at the fast-food restaurant was $4.70. John's bill at another store was $2.47."

Most beings would say this is maybe a remarkable coincidence and lay it aside at that. In this other realm that I am speaking of, however, the ever-circling amount of coincidence will continue to bring itself into your awareness. For instance, as we were dictating this, you needed to do something with a bank and a bank called, letting you know you were on track.

Many times, you have saved yourself telephone bills by thinking of another and they call you. The Law of Coincidence is the Law of Oneness, which is a higher law circumventing where you are used to living. Do you understand, then, the strange sentence that I brought out originally, that energy seeks to flow in direct reference to the subject of growing into oneness?

"Yes, the more coincidence you see, the closer to oneness you are, because there, everything matches."

Yes, and do you know that energy you occasionally feel in your head? Do you know how that works now?

"No."

It flows when the subject you are discussing or the subject I am discussing attracts energy from the universal substance, causing an opening of your gates, raising you into an expanded state, enabling you to grasp a higher principle or law. The very subject of oneness or timelessness attracts, for lack of a better word, white energy which causes you to become energetically enhanced, enabling you to perceive a greater awareness of the subject you are attempting to intuit. The more that you discuss the subject, the greater the attraction to the universal substance and it in turn flows energy to you. God is energy. This energy further works to unite others either in the same room with you or at a physical distance, who are interested in the same subject.

(The phone rings and sure enough, what Seth is saying about energy turns out to be truth, as demonstrated by the conversation on the phone.)

Now, let us get into something called the Law of Compensating Balance. We are not speaking of banking, but do you know of what we speak?

135

"No."

Each aspect or lower emotional harmonic such as anger, frustration, guilt, etc., that you let go of triggers a corresponding opening in a higher plane. True it is, as above, so below. Think how this works. You may have a friend or an acquaintance with whom you have worked out some emotional issue of which you both elected to use each other as mirrors. You both come to a meeting of the minds, so to speak, that would enable you to put out of your mind or field of attraction any further work on this emotional issue. Let us say you were jealous of some individual and instead of letting the emotion build, further delving you into the depths of time and despair, you decided to make an effort and talk over the situation directly with the individual in question. Now, this happened to you, didn't it?

"Yes."

So, you made an effort to talk to this individual, opening yourself up to allow the issue to be struck if you were both so inclined. What happened then?

"The issue never came up. The other person started telling me inane stories and we chatted until we got bored, then I left."

Would you say, perhaps time shifted?

"I don't understand."

By being willing to face the issue, you jointly "plebiated" each other and the invisible transfer of energy enabled you to let go of the jealous feeling. What do you think would happen if a similar situation came up again? Would you get jealous?

"No, I don't think so. I think the feeling I had while we were talking would take over and I would not feel jealous."

Since that time, speaking of the Law of Compensating Balances, what has happened to you?

"With regard to jealousy?"

With regard to anything.

"My life has shifted to a happier plane. When I dealt with jealously toward one person, I seem to have dealt with it in all areas. It is no longer an issue."

So you might say you have shifted axially to a higher spiral. So what you have laid aside in one plane of reality, you expand in a higher one with what you call happiness.

"Where do you get these words?"

I am compensating my balances on another plane. I thought you'd never ask.

(Seth gets up and grabs a piece of burnt-orange material and a flashlight and steps over to a replica of a triangle.)

Now, it doesn't need to be mentioned that your average American family does not necessarily have a triangle sitting around the house. But since it was convenient and in your house, I thought I would use it to prove to you the interconnection of the higher or timeless plane.

It has been stated by using burnt-orange on the phi dimension on the hypotenuse of a right triangle, it would project you into another realm of reality, a higher plane. So, I wanted to test this out. So what happened when I put the flashlight to the burnt-orange on this spot?

"I felt energy in my forehead."

Did I have any electrodes attached to your forehead?

"No."

So ordinarily, a flashlight would not cause energy in your forehead in the daylight?

"No."

Then we applied to the same flashlight another shade of burnt-orange at the eye of the triangle and what happened?

"I felt energy in my left eye."

Yes. This corresponds to the left side of the triangle or the eye of Isis. What do you think this experiment, as simple as it was, showed you?

"I don't know."

When I hit the intersection of the sacred trapezoid on the hypotenuse of a right triangle, your so-called third eye felt the pressure. And when I flashed the eye which was similar to the eye on the triangle in the King's Chamber of the Great Pyramid, you felt it in your eye. Do you suppose you are being created here through your higher mind using geometry? Or, another way of putting it, energy from the higher plane reaches your density by way of geometry by, let us say, reflection. Is this a difficult thing to believe?

"It's not difficult at all because I just experienced it. Seeing is believing."

Do you see how possibly one could create by projection, that the Law of Compensating Balances is the law of geometric projection by compensation?

"I seem to be spaced out."

Is that a triangle or a square space?

"Who cares? It feels good."

Time certainly is as you project it.

E L E V E N

OVERVIEW

"I'm really having trouble typing today. I'm so spaced out."

Think how this would be if this were a permanent condition. This would be your compartment of knowing and there would be none other. Of course, all other beings would be in a similar condition of spaced-out-edness, or is it spaced-inadeness? It is a good thing that you have time zones so that you can zone out together, isn't it? After all of this, has your concept of time changed?

"Yes."

Now, you would think I am etherically twisting your arm. What is different here?

I seem to be in a different zone or reality from where I existed previously. My revelation concerning my fitting in to existing society seems to have changed, but I can't explain how. I seem to be able to view others at a greater distance, enabling me to see more where they are coming from. Instead of being in it, I am around it, so to speak."

As you begin to realize, as you explained to me during a cigarette break, that what is happening in a verbal sense is merely a slowed down transference of energy and is really not what's happening. To make a conversation truly timeless would involve the drawing in of higher energy by willingly intending for a miracle to occur. Now, what do I mean by miracle? I literally mean a change in time by a change of mind.

You decide that something no longer is valid for you or truthful for you and so you decide in some way that it will change. You decide that, not by a force of what you might call egotistical will, but will it to change by letting go and allowing the force of divine will to mutate on a higher plane, enabling this higher energy and higher living from a lighter plane to then begin to be experienced by you.

Many times I have stated you create your own reality. Again, you would have some idea of what I mean. There are those who might say, "But Seth, I am happy with my life and I don't want to change. Do you know anyone like this?

"I think so."

What is their life like?

"Well, the person who came to mind when you asked the question, still has the same old aches and pains she had a year ago. That, to me, would indicate she hasn't changed."

So, for reasons unknown to you, the individual appears to be fooling herself. There is another kind of individual that you experience who merely wants to talk about her problem. She doesn't want to change anything and would resist your effort if you offered a suggestion of how she could change her situation. All she wishes to do is discuss the situation over and over and can hear nothing that any listener might feed back to her. It is probably boring, indeed, for those professionals who get paid to listen to such a barrage when year upon year goes by and you hear the same story.

It takes a bit of willingness to allow in a view out of the compartmentalized world that you have created around you. When you open your door and make yourself vulnerable to change, you feel the energy of making yourself at risk to switch into a different mode of operation. Maybe I could as well say, a different plane of operation. You might become invisible to those around you as you drift into constant change. How do your children view you after the changes you have experienced over the last year?

"They have said they don't recognize where I'm at."

Now, this is a switch. I thought adults were always complaining that they didn't know where the children were at.

"It's different in this family."

What do you think happens to your appearance as you constantly let go of aspects of yourself and take on new forms of expression?

"Your appearance gets better, younger."

There is this movie that was taken some year and a half ago with a group of you that come regularly to channeling. You have viewed this movie every few months since that time. What has happened to the appearance of the beings in that movie?

"They appear older in the movie than they do now."

How can this be? Where their supposedly late appearance appears younger, you included, than the earlier appearance. The only one who appears not to change at all is John, when he is channeling energy. It would appear on the surface that this is impossible but yet, before your very eyes and the eyes of about seventeen others, all witnessed the same thing. Each time you view this tape, the viewing is all that much more startling.

Over a period of your time experience, energy is flowing to you and others in a constructive way in order to assist you, with your willingness, to see that the concreteness that you have attributed to your physical density is an illusion. It is illusory to the extent that you do not see the broader planes. One of

141

your friends was explaining to someone the other day that as you look at a bright light such as the sun or a bright reflection, you may temporarily be blinded or have cell memory or what is called an after-image for a few minutes. As film is edited in your mental projector that is editing out lower emotion, your abilities as a reflector of light or this after-image, increase. They increase to the proportion that you let go of the lower emotion called opaqueness. Each, within, has a divine reflector. At one of your gatherings, a friend of yours experimented with a very large strobe light. It was approximately two feet by three feet and fired at the rate of .001 seconds. What happened when you witnessed this bright, white flash?

"After the flash, we saw different colors form at different angles."

What was the first color as an after-image?

"Violet."

What was the second color?

"Gold."

And what was the third color?

"Burnt-orange."

The first color, then, was white and it was vertical to the floor of the room. the violet was at approximately 52°. The gold was then at another angle that you are unaware of and the burnt-orange was at approximately 33°. Wasn't there a fellow by the name of Euclid who had a 47th Principle, who described this phenomena?

"Yes."

Light follows certain geometric properties. Eyes follow certain geometric properties. The properties that follow are in direct relationship to your relative density.

142

Viewing time as a fixed medium for thought has caused beings so many problems that it would take much space to elaborate. The idea of placing all emotion into a wrapped time/space continuum of sameness has contributed to the compartmentalization of feelings.

Now, a friend of yours called just a little while ago from her compartment. What was her local address?

"Rejection."

So, everyone within certain confines who would be male would then enter into her consciousness as suitable experiences of rejection. Prior to accepting this humorous sounding idea, much human suffering, including guilt, would be undergone. The intellect, using emotion, is quite clever in seeking out other beings who would be seeking to experience passing out rejection. How does this relate to time?

"It lengthens time."

What has happened each time this individual in time has experienced rejection?

"She goes further into her compartment each time."

When this sort of thing happens, she then becomes wedged into sameness, doesn't she?

"Yes."

Many beings would find themselves in this unhappy time extension and would practice avoidance of participation and would continuously lengthen the process until it was time for a new body.

What would you do if you were in that situation?

"I would do anything I had to do to raise myself above that situation."

Are many beings practicing this? Where would you begin?

"I would get interested in something else."

In other words, you would change your polarity by focusing on, let us say, your number two interest and put as much energy as is possible into that interest. You might even put a little energy into your number three interest and before long, you would find that you were bringing yourself back into balance. What else might you do?

"I would realize that I had a problem of attracting rejection and I would start the process of solving my problem. I would get into the solution. My willingness to solve the problem would attract the solution to me."

(Seth goes over and picks up the gold vase with water in it and shakes it in front of me. I am so busy typing that I hardly notice him until he holds it right in front of my face. I wonder why he is doing this.)

As we discussed earlier, if you focus on gold, then the solution is golden or higher in appearance. One caught in his compartment might say, "What good is this going to do?" and decide not to even budge. But if one were tired of the rejection mode, it wouldn't do any harm to try such a thing, for it would be better than rotting in the murky behavior.

You have run into another being today who has decided to take her will in her hands and seek to change the results in a harmful way against the ideas that her body apparently is pointing out to her.

To clarify this, let us say that there is someone who at some thirty-eight years of age with a life long history of problems with breathing, decides against the dictates of his body to be a marathon runner because he suddenly identified with marathon racing. It wasn't too long before it was realized that his body was not responding well to the idea. Breathing was not improving and the condition of his body was not improving, either. The situation here was one where probably a new interest would help to change the viewpoint of the being in question, hence a change in time was a solution, but perhaps this was not the ideal one. What would you suggest to this being?

"Nothing. I wouldn't waste my time. I don't think he could hear anything. He has already decided what he will do."

You are quite right. There is a difference between wanting help and asking for help. But there is one area that is never fooled and that is the realm of energy called the timeless. You can fool yourself with the illusory nature of lower emotion, but the higher, timeless vein will flow the energy to the one who opens the mind willingly to change. We are again speaking of letting go, aren't we?

The concept of the unknowable became so devasting to beings when the angle of the earth changed relative to the prevailing celestial plane that false pockets of illusion called the astral plane were created by beings to allow a cushion of time to overcome their fear of the unknowable. There are many lofty concepts seeking to exlain time and one of them would be relativity. The problem with these explanations and others is they did not go far enough to further incorporate other planes or reality that to a great extent, influence existing lives. This plane of reality is so small or miniscule relative to All That Is that its relative importance to fixed ideas render it into a grand illusion. Time is engendered again to allow the bite of emotion to heal where again the body consciousness through the mind can face the direction of the wind at 52°. You might say that you are sailing the celestial river as the Egyptians implied. As was stated earlier, one keeps living in time until you come to the realization that you have totally free choice. At that time, you begin to circumvent time and your life in time is limited. The concept was explored of ever evolving lifetimes where one learns the avoidance of oppressive behavior, but these lifetimes are not according to historical linearity.

You have seen from time to time, if you remember, that by use of certain lights and colors, that you can change your concept of the probable future. Do you remember when your children looked at the lights?*

"Yes, they looked at the lights and shortly afterward began to know things would happen before they actually did happen. They could see into the future."

Now, they were only interested in this phenomena for awhile and then tended to get back into their compartments of living. You might say learning is remembering.

A better way to view time is to view it as an angle of light. As the Egyptians and some other ancient civilizations viewed the calendar, they determined that the certain helical risings of particular stars such as Sirius, Alchernar and others, would signal a certain type of energy intersecting their plane of light. You are becoming aware of some of these ancient ideas again in your life. Is that correct?

"Well, I use certain stones such as carnelian and amethyst periodically to assist in attuning myself to these angles of light."

Finally, viewing time as vibrations of emotion, when overcome or let go of, bring forth a different feeling of time which we will then call timelessness. When all emotion has no further attachment, then oneness or timelessness has reached you. When you expand your vision by letting go of emotion, your viewing is extended not only in miles, but to multi-angles of light.

*The McAuliffes have a fluorescent light that has been wrapped in colored plastic and with the use of a chrystal, carefully blended to produce hues that cause the merging of energy in the head to lift someone to an extended vibration of seeing after observing the light for a few minutes. (Do not try making such a device at home unless you are an experienced electrician).

FUTURE

As the ancients have written, nothing ever stands still. Everything vibrates and never rests at exactly the same pole again. I have mentioned before that the past is slower than your present now moment and the future is faster. I hope with the reading of this book and the experimentation with some of the ideas, you will learn enough to raise your vibrations and see beyond this now moment. I have mentioned in another book of mine that you can change the past and undo all attachment to it by using the now moment. The past is out of phase with you and will cause you to incur time as we've discussed, known as emotion, by seeking to bring it forth. Your probable future in time has not arrived and you are creating it each now moment as you go along.

We have dicussed from time to time your seeing of the probable future. Do you recall any of those times?

"Yes."

In order for you to see the most probable future, you have to speed up your seeing or seeing vibrations enough to, what you might say, catch up with it. Then you might say, "Where is it?" Where do you think it is?

"Physically, right here, but vibration-wise, on a higher plane."

Yes, you are quite right. It is in your higher mental sphere of vibration. Let us say it is far reaching or far seeing.

An example of this is when John was sitting here yesterday and he thought he heard the faint sound of a doorbell ringing. He was expecting someone who had not yet arrived. Upon the person's arrival, the doorbell rang in John's conscious dimension and John let him in. You might say that John heard the future probable doorbell ring in a higher frame of vibration preceding the probable present. The higher your vibration, the more you use the higher law and you become governor of your lower plane and can learn to oversee it. Understand, as the pendulum swings as you get to the top of the arc, the vibrations ever increase until you are vibrating practically at rest. At this point, past and future are intertwined and it all becomes a kind of oneness that is immediately beyond you in your immediate present.

This is not an unreachable state and as I mentioned, the Law of Compensating Balances allows you to let go of a piece of the lower plane and replace it with a piece of the higher, so to speak.

While speaking of the Law of Compensating Balances, we need enter into a brief discussion of the Law of Rhythm. All things ebb and flow--insects, beings, worlds, stars, universes. They are created. They form. They become their most dense and slowly fade back to the beginning only to begin again. It is the constant process of death and renewal. Many have written of this.

The Law of Rhythm also fits into the category of human emotion. For example, upon some occasions, beings feel more fearful of a particular idea, let us say lack of money, than at other times. Or, another example might be you feeling more fearful of a certain kind of person whom you dislike than at other times. You might have some difficulty understanding why sometimes you are more fearful than at other times and nothing apparently is different except you. Have you ever experienced such a thing?

"I'm having a little trouble."

What about anger?

"Oh, no problem. I hate pushy, attention hungry people."

So at times you run into more of them than others. Is this so?

"Yes."

Then you have encountered the Law of Rhythm or Cycles. When you encounter this, as has been written, focus on the positive pole and steadfastly maintain your attention toward it until the Law of Rhythm causes this particular interference to pass into your lower subconscious. Do you understand what I mean?

"I think so."

Focus on the positive pole no matter what, for the positive pole is the higher pole of polarity.

It is necessary to discuss the Law of Rhythm and Cycles along with Compensating Balances in order to discuss the future. The future is some balance of the past. In this age, the focus is preponderantly on materialism, not in all parts of the planet so much as in the industrialized nations. You know that an over-focus on any particular aspect, be it food, emotion, sleep or any other habit, puts you into a compartmentalized way of thinking or being that throws you out of balance. What would happen if the demand for gold picked up and the available supply stayed the same?

"The price of gold would go up. It would become more scarce and more desirable."

149

If the demand continued, what would happen?

"You couldn't obtain it at any price."

So you would have a scarcity and perhaps what you might call gold fever, as has happened in the United States in your previous century.

Now, what would happen if beings continued to place money and technology for technology's sake ahead of all else?

"Things would be out of balance."

Then, if what I have stated about compensating balances is true, at some point there need be a swing back the other direction. There have been other technological societies on your planet, the evidence of which is quite difficult to find due to the great length of even your present time.

One of the things that would happen would be certain compartmentalization of thoughts and ideas that seemingly would be disconnected from all other elements. Little signs of stress would start to emerge, showing that the structure had become satiated and a shift was due.

Much study has been conducted by geologists attempting to understand enough about the phenomena of earthquakes to enable them to predict them. The same is true of weather patterns, with some degree of success. The ancient civilizations were also concerned with these matters, but in their case, they attempted to know the future in order to predict what their crop yields would be at a given time and if certain destructive weather patterns such as an El Nino in South America would be arriving in the near future.

One of the strange situations surrounding the present day society is its seeming lack of concern for the probable future. The ancients, such as the Mayans and others, had a calendric system that years in advance would let them know what type of a year it would be. They had some idea of what to expect from weather, economic conditions and any shifts or changes astronomically. Knowing these ideas in advance enabled them to prepare for it. It is not my way here to take on any system of government. It is my way to suggest a way of modifying your mental world so that you are out of the harmful rays of probable future expectations. Some say the future will be more of the past, but there is a limit to this way of thinking. Concentrating to again understand the ways of the ancients by seeking to have access to the higher mental planes will enable you to prepare for any contingency by letting go of probable future expectations. A strange thing will happen and that is, you will gain insight into the probable future which then begins to become fact. Making the outrageous suggestion that you don't know the probable future brings the actual future into view. Do you understand what I mean?

"No."

How many times will something have happened to you and you will say, "I didn't expect that," and it will be couched in happy terms?

"Many times."

I see by your puzzled expression that I have lost you around one of the last corners."

"What do you mean, outrageous suggestion that I don't know the probable future? I'm confused."

I thought that flew just a little too well. When you think that you don't know, then you do. Many times you have stated that, "I don't know what is going to happen tomorrow when we go to this place, but I am sure it will be fun because things always happen when we go places." That is sufficient to eliminate any probable future expectations for you would joyfully know that only something of benefit or fun would happen. You have really opened yourself up to experience joy as the universe, which includes you, would provide. Now, do you understand?

"Now I understand."

In your probable future, the spiraling energy intersecting this planet from your immediate universe is providing an ever increasing vibration of energy that would assist in raising you into a higher plane. If you decide to go in concert with it, then you will tie into an ever brightening spiral. As you have cycles as a civilization, so does your planet, so does your immediate star system and so does your universe. As you elect to go along with this ever increasingly vibrant conjunct, your consciousness will continue to be raised.

As your vibrations increase, you will gradually become aware of some of the ideas in the timeless frame that I've been seeking to explain. The concept of a clock will gradually disappear from your consciousness and you will again take charge of your destiny.

John and Dotti McAuliffe have given a new voice to an old friend, and this is certainly a treat for those of us who eagerly read the earlier Seth books by Jane Roberts. More importantly, what Seth has to say is very valuable, and he is not done yet.

Having dealt with a couple of abstract topics in their first two books, Seth and the McAuliffes will turn to some practical and specific applications in their third book, to be released in 1989.

In the meantime, we at UNI★SUN will do our best to publish books and offer products that make a real contribution to the global spiritual awakening that has already begun on this planet. For a free copy of our catalog, please write to:

UNI★SUN
P.O. Box 25421
Kansas City, Missouri 64119
U.S.A.